BANKER PONIES
AN ENDANGERED SPECIES

By Jean Day

GOLDEN AGE PRESS

OTHER BOOKS BY AUTHOR

Cedar Island Fisher Folk
Sea, Sand, and Settlers
Wild Ponies of the Outer Banks
Blackbeard Terror of the Seas

Copyright © 1997 by Jean Day
Library of Congress #97-94131
ISBN # 1-890 238-45-7

1st Printing----August 1997

GOLDEN AGE PRESS
599 Roberts Rd. 11
Newport, NC

Printed by
Griffin & Tilghman Printers, Inc.
New Bern, NC

Dedicated to the many who have fought so diligently
to preserve our Wild Ponies.

Loosely based on WILD PONIES OF THE OUTER BANKS
1988

TABLE OF CONTENTS

IN THE BEGINNING

After the winds lessened, the twenty foot waves gentled into ripples on the aqua green sea. The storm was over.

Flotsam from the Spanish galleon bobbed to the surface, almost striking a dark object which appeared to be alive. As it came closer to shore, it was obvious it wasn't a man, it was a horse, a small one, but definitely a horse. Breakers washed the animal towards shore until he recovered sufficienty to swim.

When his feet struck land, he shook his head to clear his eyes. Water sprayed over his body and ran down his legs where it soaked the white sand. His sides heaved as he struggled to breathe.

He gazed about at the wind-swept beach. His ears perked at attention, his head held high. He snorted as if trying to remember back through countless generations of enforced servitude, a time when his ancestors ran free as the deer which disappeared over the sand dunes.

As he raced along the beach, his long full mane and silky tail flowed behind, his rough shaggy coat protected him from the winter winds. His thick hard hooves made sharp indentions in the wet sand.

Further down the beach, two mares heavy with foals, joined the stallion. Ragged sails tangled with ropes dragged water-laden planks into the shallows. Other portions of the broken ship drifted about, as though undecided as to whether to come or to go. Bodies of dead men slammed against the beach then back out to sea.

So it was that a Spanish galleon joined those vessels already wrecked on North Carolina's fabled Graveyard of the Atlantic. The only survivors were three Spanish mustangs.

They had reached a yet-unnamed barrier island, a portion of North Carolina's Outer Banks, consisting of wide bare beaches with low dunes covered by scattered grasses, flat grasslands, and large expanses of salt marsh along the soundside. Dense maritime forests supported black bear, herds of white-tail deer, foxes, and other small animals. Without these Outer Islands, the coast would have been flooded and forever devoid of human and animal habitation.

As early as 4,000 B.C., nomad tribes of hunters and gatherers came yearly to the coast to harvest from its forests and its seas. But in the early 1500s, several tribes of Indians lived on the mainland and came to the islands to hunt and fish.

The horses explored the island, racing up and down the sandy beach. Occasionally stopping to munch on tender green grasses.

Several days passed, then two canoes filled with Indians landed on the shore. The Indians pulled their vessels up on the sand. The horses watched from the near-by woods as the Indians dragged pieces of the wrecked ship onto land and began clawing out nails and spikes. The Indians rejoiced because these items would make useful tools and weapons.

Its verdant salt marsh grass was and is adequate for this type of horses. The shallow sounds and marshes of the Outer Banks, while isolating and separating them from the mainland, were not impassabe for young stalions traveling from island to island, gathering satelite herds and setting up new pastures.

Soon two healthy foals were born. They grew up, reproduced, and gradually the herd spread out over the island.

This is just one theory as to how the wild ponies got on the Outer Banks of North Carolina.

Christopher Columbus, de Ayllon, De Soto, and Cortez all have been credited with bringing wild horses to North America. No doubt they did. But none of them came near North Carolina's or Virginia's Barrier Islands.

In 1524, another explorer, Verrazano, a Spaniard in the service of France, landed on the Outer Banks. His exaggerated account of the land he found, the plants and animals, sounded more like a travel brochure than the report of an explorer. He made no mention of seeing any horses. If he had seen any, he would have said so.

In 1584 England's Sir Walter Raleigh sent his first expedition to the New World, with Captains Barlowe and Amandas in charge. They landed on the Outer Banks. After two days, they went to the village of local Indians, where they were entertained with talk and food.

The Indians spoke of a ship containing white men which wrecked there about 20 years before, killing all on board.

Later Barlowe wrote of the land, "Besides this island, there are many islands, replenished with deer, conies, horses, and divers beasts."

This is the first record of horses on the Outer Banks. Since Verranzo did not find any horses in 1524 and Barlowe did in 1584, the feral horses arrived sometime between these dates. The ship described by the Indians could very well have been the one.

On Raleigh's second expedition, Lane complained about the dearth of horses. So even with those he brought, there weren't many. He left to go pirating. Both he and Grenville so abused the Indians that when Sir Francis Drake stopped off shore, Grenville left with most of his men. Since one of Drake's ships had been lost, the ships were already over-loaded. They made room for Grenville's men, but there was no room for horses. They were left behind to join those already there.

Grenville later wrote that he had stocked the new land with creatures to manure the land.

Another theory is that a French ship loaded with fine horses for the American forces in the Revolutionary War had been wrecked and the horses swam ashore. Their amazing adaptability is one of their most striking characteristics.

The horses on the Outer Banks did not all descend from the original two or three. They were added to accidentally or deliberately over the years, but the first ones seem to have been of the Spanish breed. The new ones which could adjust to the new environment, lived and reproduced. The larger horses could not adapt and died.

The horses multiplied and spread to cover the barrier islands and even swam over to the mainland. An article in the "National Geographic," May 1926 estimated there were between 5,000 and 6,000 wild ponies roaming North Carolina's barrier islands. This didn't include those off the coasts of Georgia, Virginia, or Maryland.

There have been many instances of shipwrecked horses.

John Lawson, an English explorer, map-maker, and anthropologist,who traveled among the Indian tribes of North and South America, said, "horses were fed maize by the Indians. They were well shaped and swift. Indians did not ride them--

only used them to fetch home a deer."
    Questions have been asked as to whether these animals were small horses or ponies and whether they were wild, feral or exotic.

WILD means original natural state, not easily controlled, not cultivated.

FERAL means untamed, wild, savage. When applied to the horses, it is generally accepted to mean a free roaming animal which was descended from domesticated stock, no longer cared for by man, reverted to a wild condition. Using this criteria, the horses are wild and they are feral.

EXOTIC means foreign. When applied to animals or plants it means a plant or animal not native to the land. Here is where we run into difficulty. When these horses were first found on the islands, they were believed by scientists to be native to the islands. Then for many years, the experts claimed that horses did not originate in North America, but were deliberately or accidentally brought here by the Spanish, French, or English. So they were believed to be exotic.
    But now newer information has been found. DNA tests have proven that horses had their beginnings in North America about 60 million years ago.
    The ancestors of the first horses were small, shaped like a grayhound, only about twelve inches high at the shoulder, with four toes on the front feet, three toes on the rear feet. Over the years, the horses' legs became longer and their bodies

bigger; the number of toes on the feet changed to only one.

They developed the high-crowned teeth and large chewing muscles to change their diet from leaves to grass. They became more numerous then, second only to the mammoth.

They crossed freely back and forth over the land bridge from Alaska to Russia and Europe.

No one knows why the horses became extinct in North America. Camels, mammoths, and zebras disappeared about the same time, but the buffalo and elk survived. It has been suggested that either some disease struck the horses or else the early hunters, who ate the flesh, hunted them into extinction. Others connect the loss of the horses to the ice age, which caused a change in cimate.

For over 5,000 years horses have been domesticated. Man found he could travel faster and longer on horseback than on foot. Today the only true wild horses are the zebras, wild asses, and Mongolian wild horses. The Mongolian wild horses (Przewalski) no longer live in the wild, but the breed exists.

Since horses originated in North America, they are not exotic on the Outer Banks. Man is the exotic animal, not the horse.

HORSES are defined as large four legged solid hoofed domesticated animals with flowing manes and tails, generally accepted to stand 14 hands (56") tall. The height of mustangs ranges from three to five feet tall.

PONIES are horses of any small breed. Scientists define a pony as a horse smaller than 14 hands, but there are other genetic differences as well.

The horses found on the Outer Banks are generally believed to be descended from Spanish mustangs.

The tarpan, a small grey horse with upright mane and dorsal stripe came from the lowlands of Europe. They had disappeared by 1851. Two other old breeds were the Arabian and a close kin, the African barb, developed along North Africa's Barbary Coast. Both were noted for speed and endurance, attributes needed by soldiers. But they were small, incapable of carrying the heavy armor used in Northern Europe.

They needed large strong steeds--the Norse horse,

One of the oldest breeds of horse is the Arabian. Another is the African barb, developed along North Africa's Barbary Coast.

By crossing the barbs with the Norse, the early Spanish in the province of Andalusia, created the Andalusia Horse, known as the Spanish war horse, the one Christopher Columbus and other Spaniards brought to America.

So when the Spaniards brought the horse back to America, they completed the cycle--born in America, traveled to Asia, Europe, Spain, and back to America.

Confusion has arisen because some through "selective breeding" claim to have re-constructed some of the old breeds such as barbs and tarpans. But Dr. Jay Kirkpatrick, noted expert in horse behavior and breeding, in his book, "Into the Wind," says that this is impossible because we have no way of knowing how many chromosomes these animals had or other characteristics they possessed. He says that once a subspecies or breed is extinct, it is gone forever.

As the Spanish settled the New World, they continued to bring Spanish war horses. In fact, they brought so many that the Spanish back home were worried that their stock was being depleted. Eventually they forbid exportation of the horses.

However by this time, horse-breeding farms had already been set up in the West Indian colonies of Cuba, Puerto Rico, and Santo Domingo. It was from here horses were brought to the Carolina coast and accidentally or deliberately put ashore. They multiplied and gradually spread over the coast from Georgia to Maryland.

Because of isolation, they remained relatively pure.

The time came when, in an effort to prevent the destruction of the horse herds, it became important to establish the identity of the ancestors of the horses. Usually detailed documents record centuries of breeding, but such records do not exist for the mustang ponies of the Outer Banks.

The word mustang is the English pronunciation of the Spanish word "mesteno," meaning stray and wild.

The American Mustang Association decided to use the physical characteristics to identify the horses eligible to be registered as American Mustangs.

To establish their description, they studied records made by the Conquistadors and descriptions by early American writers. They studied pictures and woodcuts of the Spanish horses made by artists during that period.

This was compared with material from South American countries who were working on programs to preserve feral horses.

Although the Registry has more detailed specifications, these are the general characteristics of the American Mustangs.

Height: 13 to 14 1/2 hands.
Weight: 1000 pounds or less.
Back: short, narrow with well-sprung ribs, some have 5 or 5 1/2 lumbar vertebrae, belly is trim.
Neck: short but longer and lighter than the heavy type horse.
Eyes: broadly set, alert.
Legs: straight with strong hindquarters.
Tail: usually long and flowing, set medium low.
Disposition: intelligent, adaptable, pleasant tempered.

The Spanish Mustang Registry is now satisfied that many of the Banker ponies are descended from the horses brought to the coast during the 1500s and 1600s. Their appearance, size, even temperament and endurance are all consistent with this breed.

HABITS AND HAREMS

Experts define the marsh pony as a small horse, larger than a Shetland pony, but not what we think of as a full-sized horse. Since they are commonly known as banker ponies, marsh ponies, or island horses, the terms will be used interchangeably in this book. They have been found in many places in the world, having been either deliberately or accidentally placed there.

The horses on the Outer Banks all seem to

have been pretty much alike in the beginning, but are now differ somewhat in the various locations. They are pintos, bays, sorrels; all un-fed, un-broken, and un-ridden. Most show a definite relationship to the Spanish horse. In the winter their coats are long and shaggy; in the summer, short and sleek. Their hooves are thick and hard. The ponies are tough, hardy and durable and can live on scant rations most horses cannot tolerate.

There have been several occasions when other horses have been placed on the barrier islands, but because of the harsh living conditions, they did not survive.

The diet of the horses must have differred considerably form the diet of those remaining there today. In Sir Walter Raleigh's time, the Outer Banks were covered by varieties of trees and other vegetation now missing.

The horses were "browsers" much as deer are "browsers." They not only ate the grasses, but also such things as thorny greenbrier stems, bayberry twigs, rose hips, sea weeds, and even poison ivy. The horses at Assteague still eat these things, although 80 per cent of their diet is coarse cordgrass.

In many places where marsh ponies still exist, there is a definite scarcity of food of any sort, but the marsh ponies require less food than most other horses. They have adjusted to this diet through the years. Those who could not adjust, failed to reproduce and died. Horses have a simple digestive system, one stomach instead of four like cows do. Much of their food goes through undigested. Horses sometimes consume their own feces to extract the unused nutrients.

Since the horses eat so much salt marsh grass, they require a great deal of water, so much in fact, that sometimes it is difficult to tell the difference at a distance between a bloated stallion and a pregnant mare. Because of the high salt content of their food, the ponies need to drink water about every three hours and urinate just as often.

The areas where the horses are allowed to graze is usually marsh or sand dunes; no fresh water ponds, streams, or springs. But ponies "have learned to dig their own drinking holes with their hooves, tapping rain runoff that is stored between sand dunes in a formation called a fresh water lense," according to Rolf Hoffman, a West German graduate student, formerly at Duke University, who studied the horses on Carrot Island for five years, finishing in 1982.

The holes slowly fill up so that "one horse may spend hours drinking there." Sometimes a horse lays belly-down on the ground so that it is closer to the water source.

When even underground water is scarce, the ponies go to the sand flat to sip thin layers of rainwater deposited on top of the salty puddles left by the tide. Apparently ponies can tolerate brackish water with one-fourth the salt content of sea water. Hoffman said he had observed ponies trying to drink salt water, but he didn't know how much of it they retained.

The rate of growth of the pony herds is quite high when compared to other large animals. The population increases from 10 to 20 per cent per year. The growth depends upon nutrition, weather, birth rate, and mortality.

The ponies have a social order controlled by dominant stallions. Each one has a harem group of mares. One stallion is dominant over the other in a dominance hierarchy. At about 14 years of age, the male is at the height of his power. The most dominant stallion grants his females most freedom. The others guard them more closely, even occasionally nipping at them. Sometimes a mare is taken over by another male by fighting or by bluffing her stallion.

One of the mares leads the harem to the water hole to drink. The male stands guard. If there are other horses at the water hole ahead of them, the lead mare will stop short.

The less dominant stallion will sometimes go forward and even half-heartedly issue a challenge to those at the water, but then he and his harem will usually stand aside and wait for their turn. There is a definite order of preference. The least dominant male and his harem must wait until all others have drunk their fill. They also get the poorest pasture, so it is no wonder that he and his harem suffer the most when there is a shortage of water or grass. The stallion does not drink until his mares are finished.

Each family or band or harem is composed of the stallion, his mares and their foals. Yet in some bands out west, there are two stallions. The stallion's ability to hold his harem together determines the size of the band. The foals of the dominant male stand a better chance of survival than the others. They are sort of a pampered upper class. The foals stand a 50 per cent chance of surviving until they are two years of age. In a mild winter, all might live, but in a severe winter, many will die. The horses eat well on the lush summer grasses to store up strength for the scant winter pastures.

Mares will fight, kick with their rear hooves to defend their foals or themselves from danger, but they are not quarrelsome.

Many mares are continually pregnant, since gestation lasts almost one full year, and they go into their cycle soon after giving birth.

The female will not allow the male to mount her unless her cycle is exactly right. When she is ready, she raises her tail as a signal to her stallion. Occasionally a mare will give birth to twins, but this usually does not produce two healthy babies at once. Since the mares usually do not become pregnant while nursing the foal, foals will nurse until they are two or three years old.

When a new stallion takes over a harem, sometimes he will attempt to kill the foals who are not from his seed. This is especially true when the foal is male, a possible later competitor.

Stallions fight more, sometimes seriously, often just for show. Hoffman states, "Their combat begins with much stooping and sniffing, neighing. The next stage--mild front hoof kicking--results in ineffective blows to the chest. In a serious fight, stallions will lock in a neck biting frenzy, rolling and kicking with all four hooves.

But one usually retreats (head hanging low) before the other."

The stallion controls his band by body gestures and verbal signals, which his mares and foals understand. When the stallion pulls his ears back, stretches his neck low to the ground and moves his head from side to side, his mares know this is a danger signal and race away, while the stallion follows behind, ready to turn and protect his herd.

Young stallions at two or three years of age are forced from the band by the dominant stallion since they are at an age to be a challenge to their leader. They usually join up with other young stallions until they are about three to five years of age and ready to attempt to take over a stallion's harem or start one of their own. If they are not successful, they wander about either alone or with other un-mated stallions.

If a stallion loses his harem, he is no longer a breeder (perhaps 16 years of age), and he wanders about another year or so until he dies.

The young mares usually leave their parent harem between one and two years of age, pushed out by the older mares. They join other harems. This reduces inbreeding. Nature seems to know how to avoid these close relationships.

At a water hole, the groups of young stallions must stand aside and allow the harem groups to drink first. So they too, suffer in a bad year.

Horses don't seem to establish territorial rights as do many wild animals and some domesticated ones. The various families wander about from place to place, steering clear of other family groups as much as possible. It is almost as if they have an imaginary line drawn around them, daring others to cross over.

Some say that if one pony gets stuck in a quagmire, others will endanger their lives to press close against his body in an attempt to push it out of the mire.

In the summer, the horses try to avoid the heat of the day by seeking shelter under trees, or by not moving about much.

It is not at all unusual to see cattle egrets perched on the back of a pony. They are a white, long-legged member of the heron family which helps the ponies fight biting flies and ticks by eating them off their coats and near their legs as they walk. The ponies help the egrets by walking along, munching on the grass, flushing out flies and ticks.

Students who have studied feral horses and the way they live at the various locations, seem to agree as far as the harems and social dominance order are concerned and their habits of eating and drinking.

Banker ponies ignore the rain, but detest the wind.

Strangely enough, domesticated horses do not have the same social habits as the wild ones do.

Hoffman said he once visited a horse farm near Durham, where he attempted to induce feral-type behavior in a domesticated stallion. He was unsuccessful.

He also batted zero when he tried to persuade

some Bird Shoals ponies to drink from a water bucket. "They never drank it," he said. "When I put it in a water hole, they dug around the bucket. They did not appreciate human interference at all."

Shackleford Ponies by
© Frances A. Eubanks Photography

CARROT ISLAND

by Robert Day

Johnny went to Carrot Island,
To film the Banker Pony.
He needed the perfect habitat,
To record it on his Sony.

But what Johnny found when he got there,
Was a barren patch of sand;
The Army Corp of Engineers,
Had covered up the land.

CARROT ISLAND: RACHAEL CARSON ESTUARINE SANCTUARY

Bordering on Taylor's Creek, across from Front Street in Beaufort, North Carolina, are several long narrow islands called the Rachael Carson Sanctuary. This is a part of the N.C. National Estuarine Sanctuary, a combination of marshes, tidal flats, eel grass beds, sand flats, and artificially created dredged spoil islands.

It's well-known for the wild horses which graze on the marsh grasses and for the more that 160 different species of birds which have been seen on the islands.

But even before these horses were put there, other wild horses came down to the water's edge or loped across the hummocks. Sometimes they swam across the creek and thundered down Beaufort's shell roads. The scarcity of food and their exposure to the elements made them tough and strong.

They were inexpensive to buy and cheap to feed, so many of Beaufort's citizens owned a horse or two to be used as beasts of burden or for pleasure.

Mr. Winfield Chadwick kept a buggy with a

SCUTTLEBUTT
433 Front Street
BEAUFORT, NC 28516
(252) 728-7765

CUSTOMER'S ORDER NO.	PHONE				DATE 1/9/08	
NAME						
ADDRESS						

CASH	C.O.D.	CHARGE	ON ACCT.	MDSE. RET'D.	PAID OUT	
1	1-890238-45-7				10	00
	Banker Ponies					
					TAX	
SOLD BY	RECEIVED BY				TOTAL	10 68

C PRODUCT 609   All claims and returned goods MUST be accompanied by this bill.

202527

Thank You

buggy horse and one or two ponies. Mr. Thomas Carrow wrote in 1948, "One of the ponies was named Sal. She had the reputation of being the smallest pony in the town, and the Chadwick boys took great delight in riding Sal. One day "Cooch," the younger son, let me take a ride on Sal. I had covered a square or two at a good clip and was going along when all of a sudden, Sal stopped in her tracks, and I kept on going. When I came to, I was lying on a couch in Mr. William Rice's barber shop."

Mr. Chadwick's buggy horse was named Grover after the President. He was a beautiful black spirited animal. Those who couldn't afford a horse and buggy envied Miss Corinne and the girls when they went on afternoon drives.

On one occasion Thomas tried to ride a pony in a boy's yard without using a bridle. It was just a childish prank. He got on the pony's back. His friend Lawrence Hassell threw a barrel at the pony. The pony threw Thomas in the dirt.

According to Thomas Carrow, Tom Noe, the butcher went to New Bern and bought a fine looking horse. He fattened him up. He was right proud of that horse. But alas, one day the horse fell over with a fit to Mr. Noe's chagrin and sorrow. Later he learned that the man who sold him the horse had had the same experience with him.

Because Rachael Carson researched the environment on Carrot Island and Bird Shoal during the 1940s and wrote a book warning of the importance of preserving coastal ecosystems, it was named after her.

To Carteret Countians, "Carrot Island" is generally accepted to include Carrot Island, Town Marsh, Bird Shoal, and Horse Island. Older Beaufort folks say that Carrot Island was once known as Cart Island, not really an island at all, but marsh a man could walk across only if he picked the higher, firmer spots. It is said to have received its name from the fact that fishermen carried fuel for their boats across from Beaufort in small carts pulled by ponies to Cart Island, where the fuel was placed in their boats.

However, early maps list it as Carrot Island. When the channel (Taylor's Creek) was dug, some of the spoils were placed on Cart Island, making it higher and more stable.

The people of Beaufort have always felt that Carrot Island and its horses belonged to them.

They enjoyed sitting in their rocking chairs on their front porches and watching the horses across the "cut" as they came down to the water's edge or loped across the islands' hummocks. Some wondered it the horses didn't watch the people watching them. If they did, they saw the transformation of a once-decaying waterfront turned into a dock for world-going sail boats, a boardwalk, and thriving small businesses.

It is difficult to say exactly when these particular horses were placed there, but it was apparently in 1954, Dr. Luther Fulcher, a Beaufort physician, whose office was on Front Street, placed six of his Shackleford Banks horses on Carrot Island. He saw that they were provided with food and water for as long as he lived. Before he died he sold them to a local man, who occasionally provided feed.

The horses lived and multiplied and were one of the main attractions for tourists to Beaufort, often visible from Front Street.

Therefore it was quite a shock for Beaufort residents to learn that announcements appeared in publications in the western part of the state, of an auction scheduled to be held in a few days—11 a.m. July 5, 1976 of about 400 acres of Carrot Island.

Residents of Beaufort were immediately up in arms at this action and quickly formed the Beaufort Conservancy Council, in an attempt to stop the sale of Carrot Island. Warren Davis, a Beaufort attorney, acted for the group and obtained a temporary restraint order signed by then Morehead City District Court Judge Herbert O. Phillips III.

Beaufort residents could not understand how anyone could obtain title to an island composed mostly of spoilage. The State Attorney General's Office and State Department of Administration began investigation to see if the state had any interest in ownership of the land.

Folks at Beaufort were offended to think that this little bit of nature across from them was in danger of becoming the site for condominiums or even factories. Since there was no way to reach the island except by boat, they feared a bridge would be built, further interfering with the image of Beaufort as a small historical fishing village, which they were attempting to create.

They learned that the land had belonged to
Harvey Smith, a menhaden magnate from Beaufort.
When Mr. Smith disposed of his fish concerns,
the Carrot Island land was acquired by Hanson
Properties, a British concern. In April 1976,
Robert Clodfelter, High Point, purchased the
land for $75,000. He then made plans to auction
it off in five and ten acre tracts.
The Beaufort Land Conservancy Council, claimed
that there was not that much land available
because of the high water mark.
The land was re-platted at 178.5 acres (land
above the high water mark). After much
negotiations and efforts to raise money, the
tract of land on Carrot Island and Bird Shoal
was transferred by payment of $250,000 by the
Nature Conservancy, a national non-profit
organization dedicated to the protection of
natural lands.
Beaufort companies, individuals, and local
organizations scurried around to provide the
necessary funds.
The agreement contained strict provisions
for maintenance of the land in its natural state.
It specifically prohibited any residential,
commercial, or industrial development.
No mention was made of the ponies.
Local citizens and companies had worked
together to protect this picturesque barrier
island, created for the most part by dredge
spoils, from being commercialized. The ponies
continued to use it as their range. Sea oats
gently waved over the sand hills, all manner
of sea life around it and on it, safe from human

habitation.

In April of 1984, a 2,025 acre plot, including marsh, sandbars, and eel flats sanctuary was dedicated as a state natural preserve, including Carrot Island, Town Marsh, Bird Shoal, and Horse Island, and called the Rachael Carson Estuarine Sanctuary, under supervision of the Sanctuary Coordinator, Division of Coastal Management, North Carolina Department of Natural Resources and Community Development.

The horses continued to entertain Beaufort residents and tourists, who enjoyed seeing the beautiful animals living so close and so free. The horses multiplied until by October 1986, there were 65 ponies on the islands.

But this was not the end of the story. It was only the beginning of the end.

Tragedy struck.

Bodies of dead horses began to be seen. Citizens were once again in an uproar. What had happened to "their" ponies? What could they do to save the remainder of them?

The "Carteret County News Times" in its August 1, 1988 issue tells the story of the death of one pony.

Suzin Osborne, who lived on Front Street and had always enjoyed watching the ponies across the way told this story. Early in May they were out in their boat, looking for the horses, when they saw three rogue males on the east end of the island. Then down by the beach they saw a shaggy looking mare and her foal. The foal appeared to be about one week old.

The three rogue males came crashing out of

the woods and chased the lone mare. Mares go into their fertile cycle almost immediately after birth, so the stallions went after her. They trampled the foal as they tried to get at the mare.

The foal attempted to rise, but the mare pushed it down, in an attempt to protect it. The water was deep. The mare placed herself between her baby and the lead stallion.

As the stallion mounted the mare, the foal's head was under water. When it was over, the mare galloped away, followed by the three stallions, leaving her foal in the water.

Suzin Osborne dove into the water to rescue the foal. She dragged it up on to the beach. The foal wasn't breathing. He was about the size of a big dog with a long neck and long spindly legs, weighing about 20 pounds.

She dumped the water out of him, then gave him mouth to mouth resuscitation. Its mouth and nostrils were human sized.

Then she felt his heart beating. The foal opened and fluttered his eyes. He struggled for life, but he wasn't strong enough.

The foal died. They worked on him for 15 more minutes, then gave up.

Usually the stallion will be there to protect his mare, but since he wasn't there, the foal died. Osborne says, "It was a classic case of survival of the fittest."

For the previous four years Beth Stevens, a U.N.C. Chapel Hill Ph.D. candidate, had studied the horses on Carrot Island for a management report for the Division of Coastal Management.

Deputy John Taggart, Estuarine Sanctuary Coordinator for the North Carolina Division of Coastal Management, and Beth Stevens came to look over the dead ponies and the remainder of the herd. They said the ponies appeared to have died from starvation and parasites.

The question arose as to who owned the horses. According to reports, Mack O'Neal owned the horses.

The officials claimed they could do nothing to aid the horses until ownership was established. Mr. Taggart, Estuarine Sanctuary Coordinator for the DCM said he thought the state owned the horses, but that Mr. O'Neal had claimed ownership.

Mr. Taggart said, "A couple of years ago, I asked the legal department to look into the ownership of the horses. One of the lawyers concluded that they were probably state property, just like the rest of the features on the sanctuary."

Mr. O'Neal said he bought the horses from Dr. Luther Fulcher and Will Dudley in 1972. He claimed he had the canceled check to prove it. Dr. Fulcher, who was in bad health, had wanted assurance that the horses would be cared for after he was gone. At that time there were about 20 horses.

One of the dead horses was taken from the sanctuary to the diagnostic laboratory at N.C. State University at Raleigh. They reported that the animal died from a combination of starvation and parasites in the stomach and intestines. They concluded that the island was over-crowded.

Mr. O'Neal disagreed. He said the blame lay with the Department of Engineers. They deposited dredge sand over one-third of the horses' grazing area and destroyed their major watering hole. Carrot Island has no fresh water ponds, streams, or springs. Fertilizer applied to the sand polluted the surrounding area, finishing the job.

Mr. O'Neal said that in bad winters, he fed the horses but that winter had been so mild he hadn't realized they would need the additional feed. "I asked the state officials about removing 10 of the horses last fall and selling them for a small fee which could be used to put battery-operated wells on the islands and for feeding programs during bad winters.

"If this removal and adoption had been done last fall, there wouldn't have been so many deaths," he said. "A few deaths of the older and weaker horses is expected each winter."

Mark Hay, an assistant professor of marine fisheries at the UNC School of Marine Fisheries, Morehead City is studying the marshes of Carrot Island.

"It is clear from our data that horses are having a huge impact on the marsh on Carrot Island," he said. "The horses are making what could be a great vegetative system little more than a sandbox with vegetative stubble here and there." [He was correct in that statement. With all that dredge sand dumped on the island, it WAS a giant sand pile.]

He claimed there were places on the island where the marsh grows freely because it is unavailable for the horses. He says it would grow waist high if the ponies didn't eat it.

"The marsh if not destroyed by the horses could attract marine invertebrates," according to Hay. The horses eat salt marsh cordgrass-the grass very important in holding the sand together. The marsh grass has three spurts of growth each year; spring, summer, and fall. But it isn't noticeable because the horses eat it before it has a chance to mature.

The State claimed that the herd got as large as 87 in the early 1980s, too large a population for the island to support. They also claimed that the large herd caused severe damage to the vegetation on the island, which is supposed to be maintained in a natural state for research and education.

The State Department of Natural Resources and Community Development announced they had taken responsibility for the animals with plans to thin the herd of 42 remaining horses to 15. It was decided that hay would be provided for the horses until some of the horses could be removed.

Twenty bales of hay were brought to the island once a week by the North Carolina Division of Marine Fisheries. The horses preferred the island's natural vegetation, but when grass was sparse, they gathered around to eat the hay.

This temporarily solved the problem.

On Oct. 28, 1988, 33 of the horses were removed from the island, with promises to allow adoption of some of them. But it didn't work out that way.

Nine of the horses were "put down" because they tested positive for EIA (Equine Infectious Anemia), an AIDS-like disease which weakens the immune systems of horses and sometimes causes death. But apparently some horses can carry the disease and live normal lives for many years.

Federal law demands that any horses testing positive for the disease, be euthanized or branded and quarantined safely away from all other horses.

When asked why the horses were not tested before removal, Taggart said "We weren't anticipating this problem. We had no prior knowledge it was out there."

According to Taggart, horses do not ordinarily munch off the grass at ground level. Sheep, cattle, hogs, and goats tend to pull the plants up by the roots. But the horses munching on the grass, causes stress to plants, causing the roots to become more developed. A shift in the type of vegetation occurs.

Left alone, animals seem to have a wonderful ability to adjust their numbers to their environment. When crowding occurs, they only produce enough offspring to repopulate, replacing those who die. Those strong or best suited to the environment survive; the weak die.

The U.S. Corps of Engineers has an easement allowing them to deposit spoils on these islands when they clear the channel of Taylor's Creek. This builds up the islands, which may be a good thing, but it interferes with the grasses and the nursery area for countless sea creatures and birds which is the original purpose of the estuary system.

Most folks in Beaufort worried that the state agency wanted to remove all "their" ponies. They resented interference. They said that if man had not destroyed their environment, nature would have taken care of the over-population problem. When water or pasture is scarce, the strong live and the weak die.

But this would have been a cruel thing to allow. It would have meant countless long-suffering deaths, not just once, but over and over again. We are too civilized to sit quietly on our front porches or drive down Front Street and watch sick and dying ponies across the "cut" stumble and fall.

The state reduced the herd to 19.

Then the Division of Coastal Management instituted a birth control program. Many townsfolk were skeptical about the authorities using this drug, fearful of its reactions. Would it kill the horses or would the treatment be irreversible?

The drug—anti-LHRH—was administered to both male and female horses. They received their first birth-control shots in January, 1996. A two year $25,000 program was instituted for 1996 and 1997. The animal was not caught or tranquilized. A dart was fired into each animal, the dart hit· the horses' skin, triggered a spring loaded plunger, which injected the drug. The dart fell away, was collected, sterilized, and used again. The horses showed no reaction. Boosters were given the following spring, then again in April of 19C7. By that time the herd had increased to 37.

It doesn't take a mathematical genius to figure out that with a herd of only 37 horses, within a short time, in-breeding will occur.

The plan seems to be working. Foals are still being born, but fewer.

It didn't kill the horses. It will take years to prove if it is reversible, or if it will gradually decimate the herd.

So at least for now, it is possible for Beaufort citizens and tourists to view their "wild ponies" from Front Street and Taylor's Creek in Beaufort.

Carrot Island is accessible by private boat and by a ferry service from Beaufort. On the fragile ecosystem, the influx of visitors probably does more damage than the horses ever did.

Carrot Island Ponies
Robert Day

Shackleford Ponies by
© Frances A. Eubanks Photography

PONY PENNINGS

An account written in the "Carolina Watchman" published May 18, 1858, states: "Tradition says that Sir Walter Raleigh's men found horses on the Outer Banks and that he had some imported to England, whether as a curiosity or for crossing with the English stocks, we are not informed."

So Raleigh's men on the first expedition must have rounded up some of the wild horses.

In 1585 on Raleigh's second expedition, Grenville bought and traded for some mustangs from the Spanish at Hispanola.

When he left to go pirating, the Spanish mustangs remained behind on the Outer Banks for Lane's use. Since Lane lamented the lack of enough horses, he rounded up some of the wild horses already there.

The earliest mention of the banker ponies tell in colorful terms the story of pony pennings or round-ups. Sometimes someone would catch one of the wild ponies and tame it to pull a cart or plow or to ride.

There is no specific date when the horses stopped being just "wild " and became private property, carrying the brands of the owners. They grazed on common pasture, so round-ups were held each year in most of the places mentioned in this book.

The pennings varied in different locations, but the purpose and plans were similar. The horses were gathered up and penned to make an estimate of the number of horses and to brand the young colts, who clung closely to their mothers, so received their brand.

Some of the horses were sold, either in a direct sale, or by auction. Also the owners sometimes took out horses for their own use.

First they had to build a strong pen on a point of land jutting out into the water, leaving the land side open so the ponies could run into it.

Pony pennings were held in summer and attended by large numbers of people, who enjoyed the sight immensely, and in a small way took part in it.

Mounted men went to the far end of the island

and surrounded the first group of horses, driving them towards the enclosure. As they went along, they gathered up other hands, chasing the horses ahead, making a complete sweep of the area.

Sometimes a stallion tried to escape with his harem. The spectators cheered him on, admiring his daring, but mostly the people remained quiet, so as to not frighten the horses.

The drivers yelled and cracked their whips, urging the large herd into the pen. The spectators, who had formed a sort of wing on either side of the pen, then closed ranks, and shut the gate.

"The ponies trembled with fright, pushing themselves so closely together in one end that it was not uncommon to see one pressed up above the rest and floundering on the backs of the herd," (Carolina Watchman).

The next job was the most dangerous of the whole undertaking. Someone had to go into the pen of wild horses and catch the yearling or foal to be branded. The horses milled about, not accustomed to being handled. The "cowboy" caught the horse by the neck or head, sometimes getting kicked for his effort. By sheer physical strength, he dragged it out.

Men held it down while another branded it with a hot iron much like they did in the old west. Each owner had his own brand, registered in the county courthouse. The same brand was used for both horses and cattle.

Often the horses were gentled before being taken to the mainland. A halter was placed on the horse and a rider attempted amid the cheers and jeers of the on-lookers to ride him. A favorite method was to take the horse to a near-by creek with a muddy bottom, the mud deep and stiff enough to fatigue the horse and render him incapable of making more use of his feet than to struggle to avoid sinking too deep in the mire. Under these difficult circumstances, he soon yielded to his rider, and rarely afterwards did he resist.

But usually the owner tried to make friends with his horse to tame it. He fed him sugar or molasses or grain, talked to him and petted him. Slowly the horse was tame enough to be ridden.

Taking the horses to the mainland was not simple. Sometimes they were taken, tied and held down, across in small boats, two or three at once. Other times, flat barges were used. The ponies were easily excited, so in rough weather they often tried to escape, causing damage to the boat or to the men.

Since the horses were not accustomed to eating grain or drinking from a container, they had to be weaned from their salt grass diet to hay, and water provided in a hole in the ground. Some died of starvation, never adjusting to their new diet, but the owners were experienced men who usually tamed the young yearlings without too much difficulty. The older ones were more often a problem.

There are many stories of horses who were taken to the mainland who returned to their home. A man from Carteret County bought a young pony at Ocracoke and brought him to the mainland.

The horse escaped and the owner saw him again some time later, at Ocracoke, back on his windswept bar. The pony had waded and swum six miles to Shackleford Banks, crossed Barden Inlet, rounded Cape Lookout, traveled up Core Banks, crossed Drum Inlet, followed the shore to Portsmouth Village, and crossed the dangerous Inlet to Ocracoke—an incredible feat.

Another horse taken to Atlantic, swam eight miles to get back to Hog Island. Horses sold on Ocracoke and taken to Portsmouth reportedly returned to Ocracoke.

The "Carolina Watchman" tells of a physician who had a large practice who made his rounds on one of these ponies. After doing a day's work, the doctor turned his horse loose to graze on the common pasture. The next day, the horse was ready for another day. During those five years, the owner never fed him any corn or fodder.

The doctor used this horse for five years, then sold him for a large price.

Most of the horses used in the early communities near Chincoteague, Currituck, Ocracoke, Portsmouth, Core Banks, and Shackleford Banks were these marsh ponies.

OCRACOKE-HATTERAS

Citified lady and Old Jerry tangle over lady's straw bonnet.

OCRACOKE-HATTERAS

Ocracoke Island, the southern most barrier island of the Cape Hatteras National Seashore, lies about 30 miles off the mainland of North Carolina. Besides being an island, Ocracoke is also an inlet and a small town of about 600 residents.

For hundreds of years, the only contact those living on Ocracoke had with the rest of the world was by boat. It still is, but since 1957, the boats are ferries. The southern end is connected by ferry to Cedar Island and on to the mainland. The northern end is connected by ferry to Hatteras Island and up the Outer Banks to the mainland.

The name Ocracoke is believed to have come from the name Wokokon, a small tribe of Indians who lived up the Neuse River and came down and across the sound for oysters, clams, and seafood feasts.

When Raleigh's first expedition came to the Outer Banks, they stopped at Wokokon, where they found wild horses, the first record of horses on the Outer Banks. At this time, Ocracoke included Portsmouth Island. Gradually the name evolved with various spellings until it became Ocracoke.

Another theory is that in 1718, Blackbeard

the pirate, the night before his death, cried out, "Oh Crow Cock Crow," knowing that with the crowing of the cock, dawn would come.
It was, however, a sad day for Blackbeard, since he was killed there by Lt. Robert Maynard.
Lighthouses have been constructed at both Hatteras and Ocracoke to help protect shipping from the dangerous coast. Hatteras Banks is known as the greatest wreck area of the Atlantic coast. It is said that Hatteras' chief import are its wrecks.
Even before Blackbeard's time, we find the name Wokokon on maps applied to the stretch of sand reefs below Hatteras.
For awhile Ocracoke Island was not included as a part of any county, so had no taxes or responsibilities. It was attached to Carteret County in 1770, where it remained until 1845 when it became a part of Hyde County.
John Lovick and his wife received Ocracoke as a land grant. In 1733 Richard Sanderson obtained the island. At his death, his son Richard received, "Ye Isle of Ocreecock, with all the stock of horses, sheep, cattle, and hogs." So this proves that in 1733 there were horses on Ocracoke Island.
Where did these horses come from? Ocracokers say that when European ships came to the New World, they brought horses and cows. They needed the horses as beasts of burden and for riding. If a ship ran aground, the livestock was thrown overboard to lighten the load. This aided in getting the ship re-floated. Because of the difficulty of getting them back on board, often the horses were left behind.

In 1747 Spanish pirates, mostly Mulattos and Negroes, landed on Ocracoke. Several people were killed, ships were burned, and cattle, sheep, and hogs stolen. Possibly the pirates, to make room for the stolen livestock, left horses on the island to join those already there.

Ocracokers say that in 1861, a ship containing a circus troupe, coming from Havana to new York, was wrecked in a "Black Squall." All humans on board were killed, but two beautiful Arab horses swam ashore. They had plaited tails tied with wide silk ribbons. The townsfolk named them Nero and Zero. Nero liked to go in houses, stick his nose in cooking pots over fireplaces and help himself until the owner chased him out. Then he would prance and perform his circus tricks for any who would watch. Nero and Zero roamed over the island for many years, mixing with the wild ponies.

Until about 1900 no efforts were made to fence in the banker ponies which had increased until they were becoming a nuisance to the growing number of settlers. Then both national and state legislation began to be passed in an attempt to control the ponies and other livestock on the North Carolina Banks. Local residents were behind the move since they felt that the ponies were becoming pests, wandering about where they pleased, destroying gardens and yards, making a mess.

In 1939 in a book written and compiled by WPA of N.C. said, "On Cape Hatteras, wildlife is abundant. For years herds of wild horses, cattle, and hogs ranged at will until the Federal Program of Grass Plantings necessitated a strict stock law."

On Hatteras, during the days of the U.S. Lifesaving teams, the banks horses were at their best. The fearless men and their beasts walked the beaches at night, watching out at sea for a sign of a ship in distress. As vessels tipped and tossed at the will of the angry sea, the men and horses dashed into the waves to rescue the frightened seamen. When the surfmen approached the shipwreck, the horses stood at attention, waiting to pull the lifeboats back to shore.

Surfman Rasmus Midgett and his horse single-handedly rescued the crew and passengers of a schooner, swimming back and forth from ship to shore in their rescue mission. The sailors gripped the horse's thick mane and held on as the horse headed toward the beach.

In 1938, the county placed a bounty on the few remaining wild horses.

The ponies on Hatteras Island were penned in, sold, or moved first because there were several small communities who protested the marauding animals. Since there was only one small village on Ocracoke and one on Portsmouth, there were fewer complaints and more space for the ponies to graze, and the ponies were spared a little longer.

Oddly enough, legislation against the ponies was fought by the National Audubon Society, who felt the ponies were natural habitants so should not be removed. At least 10 years before DNA tests proved horses were native to the United States, the question was raised whether the horses and ring-necked pheasants were exotic, since they were there before the settlers.

Since such a large area was impossible to fence in, the islanders began selling the horses at public auction.

About 1925, a valuable stallion colt called Beeswax, whose father was one of the best polo ponies in America, was brought to the island to breed with a group of Ocracoke mares to produce a new breed of polo ponies. This produced excellent ponies: tough, intelligent, great for riding and working. Because they were soon sold off, their arrival made little lasting influence on the herd.

The 4th of July round-ups were a big success. Crowds of people attended, not only to buy horses, but for fun and entertainment. The usual price for the horses was between $50 and $100. Local men rode horses (later they used Jeeps) and herded the ponies down the island into a corral near the harbor. New colts were branded and sometimes a few of them were sold. The ponies remained penned up for a few hours, then were turned loose to wander where they pleased over the island.

In 1939 there were 50 to 100 ponies on Ocracoke, about half of them wild, the others broken for riding.

Big Ike O'Neal of Ocracoke sold some of his horses, including one he called "Old Jerry" to someone on Portsmouth Island. Imagine Big Ike's surprise when two days later, he saw Old Jerry on a high sand dune at Ocracoke munching sea oats. To do this, Jerry had swum a mile and a half across the inlet where tidal current fought the ocean swell.

He just wanted to go home.

Jerry was quite a character. He liked the ladies' straw hats. Not to wear--but to eat. One day when a lady from the big city lost her bonnet, she finally found it. The only problem was that Old Jerry had eaten half of it.

During WW II the Coast Guard kept a small band of banker ponies to patrol the beach.

Until 1959 the ponies roamed without restrictions, a natural corral and common pasture.

No one seems to know when pony ownership was established, but they were branded by the owners. The brand had to be registered with the Register of Deeds Office at Swan Quarter. The charge was ten cents. When setting up the National Seashore, National Park Services banned free grazing on Ocracoke.

In the middle 1950s, Marvin Howard, a retired sea captain, returned to his home at Ocracoke. He decided to combine some of the wild ponies with some of the young boys into the only Mounted Boy Scout Troop in the United States. He began with 15 boys and 10 horses. Each boy had to work at odd jobs to pay for his horse. Then he had to catch it, which was not an easy task, since the ponies were as at home in the water as on land. Teaching them to eat oats and hay was difficult. The scouts helped with pony pennings and marched in parades.

After a few years, the original boys grew up and the younger ones lost interest, so the troop dwindled away. In 1962 when upkeep faded, the ponies were turned over to the National Park Service.

In 1974 Ranger Jim Henning and his wife came

to Ocracoke. Until this time, no effort had been
made to keep records of the horses. The Ranger
saw to it that the horses received medical
attention and proper food. Then he attempted to
prove the origin of the horses. He identified
several physical characteristics of the Spanish
mustangs in the horses. They have fewer lumber
vertebrae than the average horse, have five to
ten times greater bone density than most horses
and are able to carry heavy weights. Their wide
foreheads and short, strong necks and beautiful
flowing manes and tails are also characteristic
of the Spanish mustang.

The Ocracoke ponies are a traditional part of
the Ocracoke picture. Today they are kept in a
180 acre fenced-in enclosure to protect and
preserve this important part of Ocracoke's heritage
as well as to assure protection of vital dune
grasses. They are furnished with feed and water
and are cared for by veterinarians, so are no
longer really wild. In fact, Ranger Henning
sometimes rode one of them while doing beach
patrol, to the amusement of the tourists.

The semi-wild ponies in the pasture give tourists
going by on the highway a glimpse of the relatively
purebred ponies living in a natural state.

Ponies have been known to swim the inlets,
although the water at the one end at Ocracoke
is both deep and swift. The herd of between 25
to 30 ponies is cared for by the park rangers,
safely away from the highway.

Today the village of Ocracoke, sprawls about,
unrestricted, old buildings and new side by side,

combining the past with the present. Ocracoke
has come a long ways from the simple, isolated
fishing community it once was, yet it retains
much of its original charm. Many tourists come
from the ferries to wander about, maybe eat lunch
at a local restaurant or shop a bit in one of
the gift shops. Before they go on their way, they
hope for a glimpse of the Ocracoke ponies, a
remnant of the 300 to 500 ponies which once roamed
wild over the island.

Ocracoke Ponies
Courtesy of Alice Rondthaler Collection
Ocracoke Preservation Society Museum

Ocracoke Ponies
Courtesy of Alice Rondthaler Collection
Ocracoke Preservation Society Museum

Ocracoke Ponies
Courtesy of © 1997 Ed Sanseverino
The Lighthouse Trading Post

CAPE LOOKOUT NATIONAL SEASHORE

Cape Lookout National Seashore finally became operational despite numerous court battles and delays.

This area had been used by the public for countless generations. Natives and tourists from the mainland traveled there by boat to spend the day swimming and fishing and scrounging along the beach for shells or whatever else they could find.

Others built temporary huts or put up tents to spend a longer time. The Seashore, first authorized in 1966 by Congress, included all the islands located between Ocracoke Island and Bogue Banks. In 1976, North Carolina deeded most of the lands on Core Banks and Portsmouth Island to the United States. Other lands, especially that on Shackleford Banks was still privately owned, but acquisition by the federal government, after several law suits, was finally accomplished. Some of this land had been in family ownership for generations and they didn't want to release it to the government.

When titles to the land finally passed to the Seashore, they found the area littered with thousands of rusted, junk vehicles and a variety of shanties, shacks, and other debris.

The Cape Lookout National Seashore included Portsmouth Island, Core Banks and Shackleford Banks. There has been confusion in the past as to the location of each of these names—where one begins and the other one leaves off. This was due, in part, to the opening and closing of the inlets. There are no bridges to Cape Lookout and no paved roads. Access is by ferries and private boats.

Shackleford Banks has always been, and still is, the island about eight miles long running north-westwardly from Cape Lookout to Beaufort Inlet. The government deepened and widened Barden Inlet, allowing fishermen access to the fishing grounds at Cape Lookout Bight.

Ferry service is available from Beaufort to Shackleford.

Core Banks runs north and south from Shackleford Banks to New Drum Inlet and Portsmouth Island. It includes Cape Lookout, Cape Lookout Lighthouse in the bend, and the landing for ferries from Harkers Island and Davis.

North of New Drum Inlet is the area now called Portsmouth Island. Ferry service to the south end of the island is available from Atlantic. At the north tip of Portsmouth Island is the deserted village of Portsmouth.

From Shackleford Banks at Beaufort Inlet to Portsmouth Village on the north is approximately 55 miles.

The islands consist mostly of wide bare beaches

with low dunes covered by scattered grasses, flat grasslands, and large expanses of salt marsh along the soundside.

As directed by Congress, its management objectives, adopted for visitor use, was that it should be managed primarily as a natural area, with only that development considered necessary for preservation of historic structures, natural resource management, and appropriate visitor recreational and interpretive use.

There are basically three different areas, each treated a little differently.

Shackleford remains natural, but horses are, under duress for the present time at least, allowed.

Core Banks is kept natural but a few cabins, owned by the Seashore, have been built to be rented out to fishermen..

Portsmouth Village remains an example of the life of those who lived there. Cabins at the southern end of the island are available for fishermen.

The first residents of this area were the Core Indians, then the wild ponies. Later pirates, included Blackbeard, preyed upon shipping, while seeking shelter in the Cape.

PORTSMOUTH ISLAND

Portsmouth Methodist Church

Once a thriving port,
Then a Union post.
Now a deserted vilage,
Mosquitos love the most.

PORTSMOUTH ISLAND

Portsmouth Village is located on the northern tip of Portsmouth Island. Even before the town was settled, it was planned and authorized by the N.C. General Assembly.

It consisted of 50 acres and was established in 1753 as a port to handle the transfer of cargo. Today the entire area from Ocracoke Inlet to New Drum Inlet is called Portsmouth Island.

The growth of the town was sluggish. About 1810 Portsmouth's soil was said to have been too depleted to produce any crops but sweet potatoes and small gardens. It has been described as a giant pasture range for livestock. One man owned over 700 sheep, 250 head of cattle, and 250 horses. The grass didn't get a chance to grow, pulled up by the roots.

This was years before the ecologists had begun to worry about the ecosystem, but even then some realized that Portsmouth was over-grazed and over-stocked.

Portsmouth was known for its pine trees so tall and straight that ship builders came fro miles around to cut trees to be used as masts for their ships. Oysters, fish, and clams, as well as geese and ducks were abundant.

Beginning in the 1840s, for a period of 20 years, the community had its greatest prosperity.

At this time, the census listed 397 persons living there, mostly engaged in "lightering" and warehouse storage for commerce transported by sea-going vessels. Lightering meant using smaller boats to remove cargo from the ocean-going ships. The occupations of the men were listed as pilots and mariners. Portsmouth had a Customs Office and Tax Collector.

During the Civil War. the Union Army occupied the island and built a large hospital.

Around 1900 unsuccessful efforts were being made to fence in or remove the ponies and cattle. Gardens had to be fenced in to keep out the livestock.

This continued until about 1959 when the remaining horses and cattle were no longer allowed to roam wild.

The boom of Portsmouth was over, its usefulness as a port finished, and the population steadily declined, until in 1943 the school was closed. In 1955 the post office was discontinued and church services in the Methodist Church irregular. After the last man living on Portsmouth died in 1911, the two remaining women moved to the mainland.

Portsmouth is now a part of Cape Lookout National Seashore and the buildings are being maintained as a part of our history. Vehicles are allowed on the island except in the village itself.

When the National Seashore took over Portsmouth

Island, hundreds of wrecked cars were on the island, an offense to naturalists. Some had been left standing where they broke down. Others had been dragged near the shore where they were now partially covered by drifting sand. In a gigantic clean-up job, those not completely buried were removed, greatly improving the appearance of the island.

It might have been aesthetically correct, but stacking the wrecked cars along the shore would have helped prevent erosion and soon been buried in sand.

Although at one time, horses, cattle, and sheep grazed on the abundant pastures, they, like the people, are now a thing of the past.

The NPS say they plan to allow Portsmouth Island, except for the Methodist Church and a few select houses, to return to the condition it was before man and his livestock destroyed it.

Nature can accomplish magnificent things, but it can't bring back the large, juicy muscatine grapes, or the tall cedars and pine trees, or the deer, foxes, horses, and divers other beasts Barlowe and Amandas found there.

CORE BANKS

Cape Lookout, at the south end of Core Banks, was listed early in its history as "Horrible Headland." The sea was constantly changing to shallow shoals, creating a real danger to shipping.

About 1840, Edmund Ruffin, an agricultural scientist from Virginia, visited the Core Banks area. He reported that aside from Portsmouth, the rest of Core Banks was unoccupied except for a small number of families about Cape Lookout Lighthouse.

Core Banks, which covers a narrow strip of land, mostly sand, from Portsmouth Island to Cape Lookout was never as heavily forested as Portsmouth Island and Shackleford.

Ruffin said, "Cattle, sheep, and horses roam wild over the area. The horses are of a dwarfish native breed, with rough and shaggy coats, and long manes. Their hooves grow to unusual lengths."

According to Ruffin, "They are capable of great endurance of labor and hardship, and live so roughly that any others from elsewhere seldom, live a year on such food and such great exposure...When the Banks ponies are removed to the mainland away from the salt marshes, many die before learning to eat grain or other strange provender...others injure, and some kill themselves, in struggling, and vain efforts to break through the stables or enclosures in which they are subsequently confined...the horses feed entirely on coarse salt grasses of the marshes and supply their want of fresh water by pawing away the sand deep enough to reach water, which oozes into the excavation, and which reservoir serves for this use while it remains open."

This shows that in 1840 the banker ponies were small and numerous.

Ruffin, who was a scientist thought the horses were native to the Outer Banks.

"Twice a year,"according to Ruffin, "there was a horse-penning where young colts were captured and branded. It was colorful and exciting."

Later Ruffin was said to have had the rather dubious distinction of firing the first shot in the Civil War.

Back in 1741, George Styron received land grants for a total of 600 acres on Core Banks, Hunting Quarters, and Hog Island. He apparently lived on Cedar Island. In 1745, when he became seriously ill, he had his neighbor, William Gaskill write his will:

"I give to my true and loving wife all of my cattle of my proper mark during her life; at her death, to be equally divided among our children, also one horse and mare during her life, at her decease to be divided equally among

the children. Likewise, what sheep are left
on the Banks to be left to my wife during her
life, and then divided between the children.
Likewise all household goods, at her death to
be left at her discretion.

"To my daughter Elizabeth Styron, I leave
all the cattle in her mark. To my son George
Styron, I leave all the cattle that is called
his, after his Mother's decease.

"To my daughter Joyce Styron, I leave all
the cattle in her mark. To my son John Styron,
I leave all female cattle that is called his
own, only all the female cattle to his son John
Styron. To my son Henry, I leave all the cattle
called his own.

"I give my two sons Adonijia and Cason Styron,
the land I now live on, to be divided equally
between them. I give to my daughter Elizabeth,
a young mare."

The horses had little monetary value, but
they were considered sort of a family keep sake.

Most of this livestock was kept on Core Banks.

Once ponies could swim across the Sound to
the mainland, where they race up and down the
hard oyster shel road, disturbing the Sunday
worship services.

Mrs. Avis Gorges of Havelock, North Carolina
said that when she was a child, her family moved
over to Core Banks directly across from their
home in Atlantic and spent the summer from the
time school let out in the spring until it
started in the fall. Avis and her father and
mother and brothers and sisters lived in a small
two-room cottage which had belonged to her great-

grandfather Wallace D. Styron. The Kilbys were
their only neighbors.

The Styron family owned wild horses, cattle,
sheep, and hogs. Mr. Styron penned up three
of the wild cows in the summer to provide milk
for the family. The animals were not fed grain,
but lived off the land. If the the Styrons needed
meat in the winter, they went over to the Banks
and killed some hogs or a cow.

Avis' mother kept a garden on the side towards
Atlantic where she raised all sorts of
vegetables. She remembered especially the beans
and squash. Her father fished and oystered.

Apparently there weren't many trees, most
what Avis called Pilletaries--a low, thorny
bush.In 1917 the family had lots of sickness
and didn't go back after that.

Horse pennings were held for many years at
Old Drum Inlet and Diamond Pen off Harkers Island
and Shackleford. The horses were removed from
Core Banks, beginning in about 1932, but most
remained until the 1950s.

According to Grayden Paul, well-known Beaufort
historian and story-teller, "the ponies were
ordered off Shackleford Banks in 1954. A 1957
statute gave the state authority to remove or
confine Outer Banks ponies if necessary to
prevent damage to the islands."

It was claimed that the ponies ate the grass
the Federal Government was planting on the reefs
to keep the sand from washing away.

One of those who helped remove the horses
was Eugene Styon of Cedar Island, He said, "I
got bit, kicked, stomped on, and even rolled

on. Sometimes I limped around for days. We would run 'em down, take them to the boat, and with one pulling on the horse by the head and the other by the tail, push them on the boat. Here they were tied up. These were real wild animals and put up quite a fight."

Core Banks is now a part of Cape Lookout National Seashore, a protected area, no longer used for pasture. No doubt, the heavy grazing especially by the sheep and cattle, contributed to the destruction of some of the vegetation, which previously protected it from storms.

There are no plans at present to do anything to reclaim Core Banks. It is being watched to see if nature can undo the damage done by man.

In 1996-97 when the horses on Shackleford Banks tested positive for EIA, some folks wanted to quarantine the affected horses on Core Banks to live out the remainder of their lives.

But the National Seashore had got the horses off that portion of the Outer Banks and wasn't about to allow them to return.

SHACKLEFORD BANKS

Shackleford Banks, known for years as the land of the Banker Pony, is a short boat ride across the sound from Beaufort. Families go there to spend the day. Young people, and some

not so young, try their skill at water skiing.
Others anchor their boats and fish awhile, not
really caring if they catch any fish or not,
just enjoying the fresh salt air, the sun, and
the relative peace of God's creation.

Some prefer the sandy beaches where they lazily
sit on their lounge chairs or lie on beach
towels, relaxed, allowing the tension and cares
of their daily lives to drain from tired bodies
as sweat soaks the dry sand.

Children splash in the shallow water, dig
for clams or search for sand dollars.

A picnic lunch is spread out under a scrub
oak tree, and everyone eats a huge meal,
appetites whetted by the open air. Trash is
gathered up to be taken back with them and
disposed of later.

Sometimes the more ambitious ones walk along
the shore, search for souvenirs, a shell, piece
of driftwood, or maybe even a relic of the past
when a few hardy fishermen and their families
lived on the deserted island. A vine covered
cemetery cradles the bones of those who never
left their beloved island.

A herd of Banks ponies munches on tall grass.
A stallion stands on a sand hill, warns his
harem of the human intrusion, then turns and
gallops away in a cloud of dust following his
mares and foals.

Shackleford is the only one of the three Cape
Lookout National Seashore Islands where wild
horses are still allowed.

Occasionally three or four horses swim or
wade across to Morgan Island, a tiny island

off Harkers Island.

Recently on a visit to Shackleford, we watched the horses, poetry in motion, so fleet and free, manes and tails flowing behind them in the wind.

When we look at Shackleford today, it is difficult to believe that people once lived there, but they did.

At one time it was heavily forested but no more. Men came over from Beaufort and cut down live oak and cedar trees to be used as timber for the construction of ships and homes.

No one knows when people first settled on Shackleford Banks, but quite a few families lived there. In the late 1890s a couple of storms came over the beach and flooded gardens, seeping in several homes. People talked about leaving. Some bought lots in the "Promised Land" near the waterfront of what is now Morehead City.

In August 1899, a severe hurricane came and water washed over everything. Houses were surrounded by water. Gardens and graveyards were ruined. The tide cut the beach low in places so every high tide washed over the sand.

It was definitely time to move. The people feared the next storm would kill them all.

Some houses were torn down to be moved, others cut in half. Some were moved whole, using two boats joined together by big planks, much like twin-hulled barges.

So Shackleford was deserted except for the wild ponies, cows, and goats. Just a few low-growing bushes and wind-bent trees to remind us of the forest which once grew there.

After Cape Lookout was purchased by the state of North Carolina, it was donated to the National Park Service as a "wilderness area." Hundreds of sheep and cattle and goats were declared as exotic animals and removed. According to the Park Service, in the late 1980s, the horse herd numbered from 80 to 100. But by 1995, the herd had increased to an estimated 224. They claimed that the animals were undernourished. Rickard of the Park Service said that EIA might be a problem. Television news programs made it sound as if the horses were starving to death.

The Park Service said they considered three alternatives to deal with the horses on Shackleford Banks:

1. Doing nothing and allowing the herd to grow unchecked.

2. Removing all the horses.

3. Or the plan they eventually decided upon. The feral horses were to be herded into holding pens and tested for EIA. Those testing positive would be destroyed. The disease-free horses would be brought to the mainland, quarantined for 60 days, then tested again. Fifty or less would be returned to the island and others adopted out.

If the authorities were surprised at the outcry about the Carrot Island ponies, they must have been shocked silly at the commotion their plan for the Shackleford ponies caused.

The citizens were convinced the National Park Service really planned to get rid of all of "their" wild horses, since they had mistakenly classified them as "exotic."

Letters to the Editor appeared in every newspaper. Petitions to save the ponies were signed by hundreds of citizens. Letters were written to state and federal officials. News crews went to the island to film the horses.

Bill Harris, superintendent of Cape Lookout National Seashore, was said it have written a letter to Senator Helms stating, "Cape Lookout National Seashore ONLY has the management responsibility for the horses on Shackleford Banks."

Mr. Monroe Paylor of Harkers Island said he'd spent many hours on Shackleford Island when he was young with his brothers and father clamming. "We were getting 40¢ a bucket," he said.

One day when they reached the Banks, they found one of the horses stuck in the mud. The poor horse must have thought it was bottomless muck. Mr. Paylor and his sons cautiously approached the horse, trying to figure out how to free it, yet not wanting to get stuck too. They worked at that pony all day long. Finally late in the afternoon, when they were about to give up, they got it free. They didn't mind that they hadn't caught any clams or made any money that day. Paylor said they felt a kind of ownership of those horses and wouldn't let one die if they could help it. "We still feel a kind of ownership," he said, "like we should be able to help take care of them."

That's the way many of the folks in the county felt. They complained about it to anyone who would listen.

They were not alone. According to the "Carteret County News Times", two nationally recognized animal scientists expressed serious reservations about the NPS controversial plan to thin the pony herd at Shackleford. Dr. Jay Kirkpatrick a director of science and conservation biology at ZooMontana Regional Zoo of the Northern Rocky Mountains and Dr. Allen Rutberg, senior scientist with the Humane Society of America, who had together successfully instituted the birth control program at Assateague, spoke up.

Dr. Kirkpatrick expressed several concerns about the Shackleford Banks horse plan.

1. He said the Cape Lookout National Park Service spoke about environmental damage, but provided no evidence.

2. Aside from the birth control component, the plan lacked detail of how the herd would be protected, even with the contraceptive, and failed to show how the genetic diversity of the herd would be preserved.

3. Any "sudden removal" of parts of the herd in a round-up would "create hardship for the horses. They are an incredibly social animals and are aware of a sense of loss."

4. According to Dr. Kirkpatrick, Cape Lookout's referral to the horses as "exotic" or foreign to the specific place is "scientifically inaccurate" and the Park Service embarrasses itself when it does that. The horses are native wildlife.

Dr. Allen Rutberg says he fears the Cape Lookout plan is running away with technology without the involvement of the Humane Society which used the drug in the management plan at Assateague Island. "If they are not going to manage for long-term survival, what are they trying to accomplish?" he asked.

Perhaps mistakenly so, but the general consensus seemed to be that NPS was intent on destroying the complete herd. It was reported that one of the "big boys" in Congress said, "all the horses on Shackleford have to go."
Some speculated that this portended a plan to commercially develop Shackleford Island.
The horses were not malnourished. A fenced-in area at the island had a sign explaining that inside the fence was the vegetation as it would be without the horses. Inside the fence, the grass was barely visible above the ground, looking dried and withered as if not fertilized.
Outside the fence, the grasses were knee-deep or higher. Manure and decayed matter produced by the horses had fertilized the land, allowing the growth of sufficient vegetation to support the horses.
Many pointed out that although the Cape Lookout

Park Service had had the ponies for ten years, they had done nothing for them, had spent no money caring for them. But now, with its budget of $1.2 million a year, they wanted to spend hundreds of thousands of dollars to destroy the herd.

Some feared that their original plan would have destroyed the gene pool in a cut so drastic that the ultimate extinction of the herd would be the consequence.

These ponies which had been on Shackleford Banks before the white man came—these ponies both residents and tourists value so much—would be gone. What hurricanes and tides and disease could not destroy, the government could and would.

The NPS has all the 50-odd miles of Core Banks. The horses there are gone. The grasses have not built up. The trees have not grown. It is a desolate land with nothing there but the NPS and a few nutrias (a truly exotic animal from South America). The land by itself cannot repair the damage done by man.

The people need the horses to remain on the Banks. The NPS wanted to remove them because they were an "exotic species." Their class-ification of wild horses as exotic is making it more and more difficult for wild horses to survive the Park Service, both here and elsewhere.

Because of the loud public outcry, Rep. Walter Jones, who represents North Carolina's 3rd Congressional District in Wash-ington, D.C. reached an agreement with Cape

Lookout National Seashore Director Bill Harris, Park Resource Manager Dr. Mike Rikard and NPS Washington official Jerry Johnson. Since there were approximately 100 horses on Shackleford and Core Banks when the Park Service took them over, it was agreed that the number to be left on Shackleford would be 100.

In November of 1996, the NPS used a combination of aerial surveillance, herding dogs, horses, and all-terrain vehicles to pen the horses. A total of 184 horses were rounded up. Two were killed during the round up. Over night the remainder were tested for EIA. The public was informed that 76 of them tested positive for EIA. Dr. Rickard said, "We were shocked when such a large number came back positive." Yet he was the one who had predicted it.

When local organizations fighting to protect the Shackleford ponies heard about the doomed horses, they suggested that they be placed on Core Banks to live out the remainder of their lives. The NPS immediately nixed the idea.

Some of the leading protesters made plans to take the ponies and made arrangements for a place to isolate them in 1,200 acres on Davis Ridge off Core Sound.

State vets declared the location unsuitable to protect uninfected horses from contracting the disease. Without allowing the group time to find another location, the state went ahead with their plans.

Jerry Hyatt of a local activist group, "We the People," followed the over-crowded trucks 100 miles away to the stockyards at Clinton,

N.C., where he waited until the deed was done.

The NPS and state vets claimed the horses were killed by lethal injection. Hyatt believes they were either shot or hit with stun guns.

This left a total of 108 horses on the island.

Families had been broken up and mares killed. Babies were left without any means of support.

The foals depend wholly on mare's milk for sustenance the first two weeks, and need it to supplement their diet for the next year. Mare's milk also builds up antibodies against disease and satisfies their thirst. The foals need their mama to show them what food is safe to eat and what water is safe to drink.

According to Elizabeth Loftin, who has had horses all her life and watched these horses on Shackleford for many years, there are plants growing on Shackleford Banks "as deadly as a shotgun blast" to the foals. Yucca trees are one of those plants. And the bits of grass the babies managed to eat was not sufficient for survival. Because of neglect, at least three of the foals died a horrible death by starvation.

The government caused this tragedy by its deliberate neglect.

Yet if a private individual left a litter of week-old puppies alone in his back yard without care or food or water, causing their deaths, that individual would be publically villified and arrested.

EIA is contracted by bites from mosquitoes, horse flies, and stable flies. It is at the present time, incurable. These horses had probably had this disease for generations. Many of them appeared perfectly healthy.

NPS claimed that since they tested positive, they were probably chronic carriers, sort of like "Typhoid Mary." The incubation period of EIA is unknown, but is believed to be from 60 days to one year.

Federal law outlines the treatment of horses testing positive for the disease. They must be either killed or quarantined safely at least 200 yards away from all other horses. Vets said that the narrow strip of land four miles from shore would effectively quarantine the horses. But the NPS disagreed.

The disease is not as easily spread as some would have you believe. If a horse fly bites an infected animal, it can only spread the disease to another animal if it bites it while the blood is still wet on its mouth. Since it only takes seconds to dry, this is far too short a time for the horsefly to fly off the Banks and bite another horse elsewhere.

Another cause of illness and death among the horses is internal parasites. Horse experts have discussed ways to manage this, but they have not found the answer yet. De-worming the horses could kill them because dead parasites would block the intestines. It is a difficult problem. Most older horses are acclimated to the parasites as well as the EIA.

It is questioned as to how much management these horses should receive. They could be managed to the point that they are no longer wild. On the other hand, we don't want to see them suffer and die. There has to be a happy medium.

The second round-up of the wild Shackleford ponies netted 103 of the herd. This time it was anounced that five tested positive for EIA.

As a result of the public relations nightmare before and after the first round-up, a non-profit organization, "Foundation for Shackleford Horses" was formed to provide management of free roaming horses in the seashore.

A tentative agreement was reached between the state and the foundation. The horses which tested positive were to be removed to a site on the mainland to spend the remainder of their lives in quarantine at Williston, NC. The stallions were gelded and all were branded.

Had the NPS not agreed on this site, the animals would have been killed. The site consists of 192 acres, five of which are fenced-in, according to Margaret Willis, foundation director. "We've made $9,000 worth of improvements. The access old logging road is now in excellent shape. The pen is turnkey and we're just waiting for the horses. The fencing is quite expensive and substantial and it's way over-built. But it's to ensure these horses cannot escape."

A TV news broadcast said that a group of horse owners from the mainland met, objecting to the infected horses being left alive, even though quarantined. They were informed that this is legal and has been successfully done in Florida, where hundreds of infected horses have been quarantined, causing no problems.

The horses are important. They are a part

of history and worthy of being saved.

Carolyn Mason is one of those who has been very active in efforts to save the Shackleford ponies. Mrs. Mason has announced that 60 examiners from the Spanish Mustang Registry from Wyoming, Colorado, Maine, and 15 other states examined the horses and removed some for a more detailed examination. They were then registered in the Spanish Mustang Registry, attesting to the fact that they are descended from original Spanish mustangs which were brought to the New World in the early 1600s and lost in shipwrecks offshore.

Shackleford Banks is not the personal property of the National Park Service. It belongs to the people. So do the horses.

Legislation to ensure the maintenance of a herd of wild horses on Shackleford Banks was introduced by N.C. Congressman Walter B. Jones. There are three basic components of the bill:

1. The horses will be permanently left on the island.

2. The population level is to be held at 100 to 110 horses. No horses are to be removed unless the herd exceeds 110. It provides provisions for management.

3. The management would be taken from the NPS and turned over to a non-profit group. It would allow the foundation to adopt any horses removed from the island.

At this time, Rep. Jones' bill has not been acted upon.

The 1996-1997 battle between the government and those wishing to preserve the Shackleford ponies has ended in a draw; approximately 100 saved and at least eighty killed outright or by deliberate neglect.

Whether this is the last battle or merely one of a series is yet to be seen.

Shackleford Ponies by
© Frances A. Eubanks Photography

Shackleford Ponies
Robert Day

Shackleford Ponies by
© Frances A. Eubanks Photography

The Horse Race

In the early 1700s horses were important in the lives of the settlers as a means of transportation, to ease the work load, and also for entertainment. There were no roads, just paths or cart paths and no cities, just small communities.

Mr. Thornton Sawyer told this story about something which he said happened in the early days in the Goose Creek Section, off Highway 264, near Bath, North Carolina.

Some of the communities had what they called tournaments. As a part of the entertainment, they would place rings on a rod or a spear and the horsemen would gallop by to try to take the ring off the spear. If he succeeded, he got to pick the queen for the night.

Then they had horse races.

In the community, there was a man by the name of Bill Elliott, who was said to be one mean man. One year he made a wager that he would win the horse race "or he would go to hell." His horse was just an ordinary horse, descended from a domestic horse and a banker pony, but he was covinced it was fast.

On this particular day, on the path towards town, Elliott met a stranger riding a good-looking black horse.

"Think your horse is pretty fast, I'll bet," Bill Elliott said.

"Fast enough to beat that scroungy steed of yours," the stranger said.

So they agreed to race to town, about five miles away.

When Elliott came to a fork in the road, his horse wanted to go right. And Bill Elliott wanted to go left, so he yanked on the reins.

The horse skidded and reared up, throwing Elliott into the right side of the long-leaf pine tree; killed him dead.

That side of the tree died.

The other side of the tree remained alive for many years until it was struck by lightning.

The place where the horse skidded, left deep tracks in the ground. Soon folks began to notice that the tracks remained, not filling in or washing away.

No trash collected in them.

A man from down that way used to put corn in the tracks to feed his hogs, but the tracks were still there, always clean. School children, passing by, would drive sticks into the tracks.

The next day, the sticks would be gone.

Mr. Sawyer said someone fenced in the area around the tracks and planned to charge admission for people to come and view them, but it didn't work out.

Not enough people wanted to pay to make it worthwhile to keep someone there to take tickets.

Mr. Sawyer claimed he had seen the tracks himself and agreed that no trash ever gathered in them.

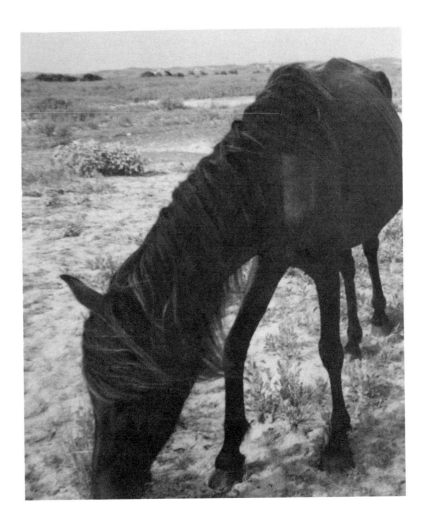

Shackleford Ponies
Robert Day

The Educated Horse   Mark Day on Ginger

  How to go to school
  Again? Of course,
  Three children riding
  On the old horse

  Morris Daniels, who lives on a farm near Stonewall, said that some time ago, he bought a horse from a man on Cedar Island.
  The horse looked good, but he had a problem. He never could train him to pull a cart. Mr. Daniels was told that this was because the horse had got salt water in his ears at some time or another. Must have given him vertigo.
  But the horse went to school.
  In fact, two different bunches of children rode him to school, sometimes three at one time, from first through seventh grade.
  Guess he must have been a real educated horse!

CURRITUCK-COROLLA

There once was a man on Currituck,
Who lived on the oysters his woman'd shuck,
No clothes did they wear
Except for their hair,
And hers blew in the wind when he had any luck.

by Robert Day

Near the top end of North Carolina's Outer Banks is a part of Currituck County where a few horses still run wild, completely unsupervised--that is--unless they stray too far north or manage to get around the fence to the south.

The name Currituck has, like so many other names along the North Carolina coast, had many different meanings and spellings over the years. It has meant all of the area from the Virginia line south to Bodie Island, a county, a sound, two inlets, a port, and the Banks.

In the past it included the small communities with such strange names as: Wash Woods, Penny Hill, Currituck Beach, Poyners Hill, Caffeys Inlet, Jeanquite, Kitty Hawk, Rowsypock, Collington, and Nags Head. More recent communities are Seagull, Deals, Corolla, Duck, Southern Shores, and Kill Devil Hills.

Those at Corolla who have studied the origin of the horses say that explorer Luces de Ayllon brought horses and other livetock he had bought at the Spanish colony of Puerto Rico to his new colony at Cape Fear. The horses were of the barb breed, originally from Portugal and Spain. Because of sickness and trouble with the Indians, de Ayllon's colony fled to Florida where the Spanish holdings were stronger. The horses were left behind.

They also mention Lane from Raleigh's second expedition as a possible source of the horses. According to Lane's journal, when their ships went aground on a shallow bar, all but one were floated off without too much difficulty. But when they attempted to bring the "Tyger" ashore, she got stuck. They struggled for two hours to prevent her from breaking up, but the corn, salt, meal, rice, and biscuits intended for the colony were lost. The livestock was forced to swim ashore. It is believed that the Corolla horses developed from these two incidents.

In the early days of Currituck, it was the home of many unsavory characters, possibly escaped criminals, marooned pirates left there to die, runaway slaves, and shipwreck survivors.

David Stick in his "Outer Banks of North Carolina," tells the story of two of these usavory characters.

A mariner who lived on the South Shore, not far from the inlet, modestly called himself a hermit. But he really had no right to that name since he had a wanton female living with him. They lived in a bower, covered Indian fashion with bark. Since the weather was mild, it kept them fairly comfortable.

He didn't believe in work. He neither plowed nor sowed any field, but survived mostly on oysters his woman gathered from the rocks. Sometimes for a change of diet, he sent her to drive up one of the neighbor's fresh cows to moisten their mouths with a little milk.

For clothing he depended mostly upon his length of beard, and she upon her length of hair, part of which she brought modestly forward, allowing the rest to dangle behind quite down to her rump.

The Poteskeet Indians lived on the mainland, but had always hunted on the islands, so even after the coming of settlers, they wanted to hunt there. Of course, this angered the settlers because they were using it as a stock range. The Indians took their case to court, and in March of 1715, the Council ordered the Bankers to allow the Indians fishing privileges.

Since North Carolina's coast is a relatively low, flat land, the early explorers had problems telling where they were. Ships often ran aground. The channels and inlets were constantly changing. To help prevent shipwrecks, North Carolina built a series of lighthouses. One of these was built at Corolla. It was first lit December first 1875.

In order for seamen to distinguish it from the lighthouses at Cape Loookout, Hatteras, and Bodie Island, Corolla's was left in its natural red brick color. Ocracoke's was of a different style.

It was a lonely job for the lighthouse keeper with only his family and the wild horses for company.

But then a few others began to move in. To support their families they both fished and farmed.

For awhile Currituck served as a port, but since no official office was established, it was soon ignored.

In 1982 only 19 people lived in a handful of houses in Corolla. The ponies outnumbered the humans. Both occupied the same land, walked the same sandy lanes and beaches. The horses considered this their home and took care to avoid the humans.

It wasn't until the 1950s that electricity came to Currituck Banks, 1968 when it came to Corolla. Telephones arrived in 1984. Finally a paved road was opened to the public, but the place was still isolated. Few vacation houses were built. Then gradually more people discovered the natural beauty of Corolla's sand and sea and fresh air. More houses were built. The sand was covered with bright golf course type green grass. To the horses this was an open salad bar. But the horses ingested fertilizer, pesticides and herbicides along with the grass.

To the horses this was their home. They were accustomed to roaming where they pleased. These strange two-legged creatures who often got in their way were unimportnt to them except for the carrots and apples they brought from the new Food Lion Store to feed them.

The horses were smart, they knew this was where the goodies came from, so one day some of them attempted to enter and by-pass the middle man. They had to be rescued.

The horses, who were accustomed to the coarse diet, now devoured the tender green grass. The band of young bachelor stallions became a special nuisance. They gathered around the covered garage in the shopping center where it was cool. Soon the smell became unbearable.

They turned over trash cans and discharged their waste anyplace they pleased.

Those who had built expensive houses weren't happy.

Horses were getting killed on the highway.

In 1989 a meeting was held and attended by

about 50 people at the village fire station to discuss the situation. They formed the Corolla Wild Horse Fund to watch over the welfare of the horses. Rowena Dorman was selected as director. They succeeded in getting the county commissioners to declare the Currituck Outer Banks a sanctuary for wild horses, making it illegal to harm, approach, feed, or kill them.

North Carolina tried to protect the horses, making it a violation to try to remove the horses, trap them, or injure them.

This gave the Horse Fund people power to attempt to teach the people and save the horses.

When the Fund came under the umbrella of the Outer Banks Conservationists, staffers Debbie Westner and Rowena Dorman went to work. They could now post signs, print educational literature, put reflective collars on the horses and diffuse dangerous situations between horses and people.

All of the horses had names. The people lived among them and felt they knew each one individually.

One day two women in their car pulling a horse trailer with horses in it drove for miles trying to find some of the wild horses. When they were stopped, one woman explained, "My mare is in heat, and I want to breed her with a wild stallion."

After a lecture, the ladies were sent on their way.

Vacationers lured a colt up cottage steps to a raised deck. The colt fell and was injured.

One of the members of the Fund, Tony Houston,

wrote in his daily journal, "one of the sorrels stuck his nose in wet concrete. I wiped off most of it with a paper towel."

The horses were wandering about, almost as pets. But not quite. They appeared tame, but they weren't. Parents had to be cautioned against putting their children on the horses' backs or petting them.

The horses wandered as far south as the communities of Sanderling and Duck.

In 1989, one car accident kiled three pregnant mares.

The Fund volunteers were constantly being called out to emergencies. Drivers ignored signs that this was a Horse Sanctuary and refused to slow down, hitting the horses.

One horse was thrown 90 feet into the air by a speeding motorist and killed.

A tiny foal drifted from its mother into the path of a passing vehicle. The rescuers tearfully removed the dead baby from the highway. The mama called all night long. "Finally she found a little bloody spot on the road and she smelled it and licked it, and all the others did too. Then they walked away," Dorman said.

"Horses do mourn, you know. When you see something like that, you'll do anything to save these horses."

Traffic became hazardous not only to the horses but also to the humans. The horses were becoming an endangered species.

The band of bachelor colts hung around one particularly dangerous spot of highway. They were chased away, but returned. The possibility of castration was discussed to make them more manageable but decided against. The horses hated to be handled and could have been injured. Finally they were loaded up into a truck and moved to the mainland.

Sometimes the injured horses were kept fenced in on the Lighthouse property and cared for by the keeper.

The community was divided; naturalist against developer, equestrians against bird-watchers, land-owners against government, and natives against tourists.

They discussed the possibility of purchasing land for a refuge, but the lack of funds and the cost of land was prohibitive. In 1994 the members of the Wild Horse Fund decided the only solution was to move the horses up to the north end of the island and construct a fence running from the sound to the shore to keep them there.

This sounded easier than it was. The idea was to eventually move the Corolla herd up to the undeveloped northern end of the island where another herd already lived. First they had to get permission to build the fence, with the stipulation that they provide a cattle guard to prevent the horses from crossing back over on the highway which passed through.

With donations of lumber and labor, they managed to cut through clinging catbriars and beat off "no-see'ems" to build a one and one-half mile fence and added the cattle guard.

In their documentary, "Wild in Corolla, the Last of the Spanish Mustangs" the Horse Fund showed how the horses were rounded up. It was done mostly by Fund members on foot with the use of walkie talkies and men on horseback. They gently urged the scattered horses up and finally succeeded in getting them all beyond the fence.

But the "cowboys " and "cowgirls" could not rejoice. It was good to think the horses would no longer be killed on the road. But to see the horses who were accustomed to running wild and free, in jail made them sick at heart.

There was already a herd of horses on the northern end of the island. Here they continued to graze, un-bothered by mankind. Well, not completely. At one time, the road could be taken on up in the Virginia part of the island. Now the road was shut off to cars. But the horses could still get through. The problem was that the ponies kept crossing over the line into the Virginia portion of the island. Then they disappeared. Some believed they were rounded up and carried off by stock truck. On one of these trips, a horse fell down and broke its leg. It was left there suffering for hours. There has been much speculation as to where those horses were shipped.

At one time it was estimated there were about 200 horses up there, but at the last count there were only 42, probably a few more because of foals born this spring.

The area where the horses live consists of 15,000 acres, 2,000 of which belongs to government agencies. It is rimmed by rolling dunes and marshes, undeveloped with no paved road.

Part of the land is the Currituck Wildlife Refuge, managed by the US Fish and Wildlife Service. The Corolla Wild Horse Fund thought the Wildlife people would welcome the horses.

But they didn't. They felt they were a threat to a part of the refuge where the piping plover, an endangered species, nested.

The Wildlife fenced in about 150 acres of its 1,800 acres to keep the horses out.

Instead of welcoming the horses, a Mr. Merritt of the Wildlife said, "We have a different view of these horses. We think they are basically free-roaming horses that were let go by ranchers years ago. Our view is quite different than those who believe the horses literally jumped off the ships and were a part of the Spanish settlements 400 years ago."

After a head count in 1995, federal authorities estimated the herd at 40 horses. Wild Horse Fund believed there should have been at least 100. County Commissioners suggested the number was more like 200. It is difficult to get an accurate count, but this is quite disparate.

Angered, the Corolla Wild Horse Fund turned to the state which oversees another 1,000 acres of nature preserve north of Corolla. The state promised to study the situation, but made no promises.

The horses who had come from Corolla missed the nice green grass and goodies handed out by the two-legged creatures. So one group managed to get around the end of the fence and returned to their home.

When the Fund members saw that they couldn't

keep the horses penned in, most of them were placed on farms on the mainland. A few with injuries and dependencies were left on the lighthouse grounds.

The Corolla Horse Fund has accomplished much of what they set out to do:

1. Worked with the veterinary department of the U of Kentucky which established by DNA testing that the horses are of Spanish origin.

2. Did genetic research on the genetic viability of the herd.

3. Implanted identification chips.

4. A census count (by air, four-wheel drive, and horseback) of the population north of HWY 12.

5. Testing for equine diseases.

6. Vet care for injured horses.

7. Fecal count to determine parasite levels.

8. Construction of an ocean to sound fence.

9. Care of the few remaining horses which could not be returned to wild because of injuries or dependencies.

10. A documentary.

11. Daily talks on the history of the Corolla wild horses during summer months on grounds of the Currituck Beach Lighthouse.

The Spanish Registry is satisfied that the Banker Horses, in particular the Ocracoke and Corolla strains, are as lineally pure to the 16th century Spanish importations as can be found in North America today, and that they compare closely to the selectively bred South

American Spanish derivative stock.

Horses isolated from other horses become a breed itself.

Moving the Corolla horses north may be at best a temporary solution. The Currituck National Wildlife Refuge will do everything they can to dispose the horses. The private land will be developed if the planned bridge is built to the mainland. This will leave the horses no place to go, something Debbie Westner and Rowena Dorman don't want to consider.

Currituck - Corolla Ponies
Courtesy of © 1997 Ed Sanseverino
The Lighthouse Trading Post

Ocracoke Ponies
Courtesy of © 1997 Ed Sanseverino
The Lighthouse Trading Post

Shackleford Ponies
Robert Day

Ocracoke Ponies
Courtesy of © 1997 Ed Sanseverino
The Lighthouse Trading Post

ASSATEAGUE AND CHINCOTEAGUE

Sand washed up from the restless Atlantic Ocean to form Assateague, a barrier island off the southern coast of Maryland and the northern coast of Virginia. Near the shore, water beat upon the land and changed the shoreline dramatically; beyond the sand dunes are forests and marshes.

Six hundred eighty acres of the northern end of Assateague Island is owned by Maryland and operated as a state park. The southern end is owned by Virginia.

Two herds of wild horses live on Assateague Island. A fence separates those in Maryland from those in Virginia. The Maryland herd is managed by the National Park Service. Across the channel from the Virginia end of Assateague is the small island of Chincoteague. The Chincoteague Fire Company owns the Virginia herd.

Folks there say the early settlers told of the skeleton of a ship put together by pegs which lay on the beach. They say it was a Spanish ship, carrying Spanish mustang horses when it was wrecked off the coast of Assateague Island. They tell the story of sailors who survived because they were helped to the mainland by the "Assateeg" Indians. It is believed that the small wiry horses managed to swim ashore and founded the herds of horses on Assateague Island.

In 1670, English settlers moved to the area and brought horses and cattle.

Others claim the horses are the remnants of herds destined for the first settlers in the Jamestown area or that the horses moved there from the South as herds expanded, searching for new grazing grounds.

In 1820 a Spanish ship, the San Lorenz, ran aground off the coast of Assateague. Horses were among its cargo. Some of the horses survived and swam ashore. The breed of these horses is unknown.

As early as the 17th century, portions of Assateague Island were used to graze horses, cattle, sheep, and goats to avoid mainland taxes and the required fences. The early settlers used Assateague as a natural corral fenced in by water.

In 1968 Assateague Island National Seashore acquired ownership of a herd of 28 feral horses. The population increased by 10 to 15 percent a year until by 1984 the count was 110.

Since the number of deaths from disease and storm is small, the herd could easily reach 250 animals if not controlled. Over-population makes inferior animals and destroys the grasses and other growth.

Dr. Jay Kirkpatrick, who spent much time studying the horses, says that he was astonished at their diet. Their main food is a variety of marsh grasses, and if left alone, they would spend their entire year munching along the tidal marshes near the bay.

But with the summer heat, clouds of mosquitoes and green-head flies invade the island and drive the horses to the lobolly pine forests. There the horses consume great quantities of greenbrier, a vine much like barbed wire capable of tearing clothes to shreds. But the horses eat it, roots, vines and all.

Since the horses are thick-skinned (unlike people) they do not suffer as much as humans do from the mosquito population. More annoying are the biting flies, which not only hurt but can cause open sores and diseases.

After the insects become absolutely intolerable, the horses move to the wind-swept sand dunes where they find beach grass and tender branches of bayberry. Finally their search for relief ends at the bay, living on dune grass. They wade out into the water, often so far only their heads are visible. On land they swish their tails in each others faces, stomp hooves, gather in tight groups, crash through thick brush, or roll on their backs in the dust to free themselves from the insects.

Spraying for insects is illegal on most of Assateague Island. However there is a two mile area administered by the State of Maryland which is sprayed weekly, so has fewer insects. When the insects get too thick on the rest of the island, some of the horse bands regularly go to this area until the danger from the bugs lessons.

Water is scarce, especially in part of the island. The horses here have been observed drinking from the bay which is not as salt as the ocean. Even the freshwater ponds are somewhat salt.

Nature attempts to take care of the survival of the herd. The insects most often bite those in the stallion group, fewer on the bearing mares, and least of all on the foals. No one knows why, but it is believed to be connected to testosterone level, temperature, and the amount of protein in the body.

When the horses eat the dune grass clumps, they have been seen swishing them back and forth to shake off the sand.

Ordinarilly on Assateague Island, the bands are not territorial. A harem band may be as small as one stallion and one mare, or as large as one stallion and 20 or more mares with their foals. The harem stallion has to be tough, aggressive, and intelligent in order to obtain and retain his harem.

Since the horses have no natural enemies except man, the numbers soon increase beyond the space available to them. With more and more land being taken from them, overcrowding caused problems to wild ponies everywhere. At Chincoteague, they solve this problem by rounding up the horses and selling off many of the foals. But on the Maryland side, as well as at Shackleford, another solution had to be found.

The mare is an unusual creature because her breeding season begins almost as soon as her foal is dropped. Gestation is approximately 340 days, so unless she nurses her young, she is almost always pregnant.

Because of the sale of the foals, 75% of the mares at Chincoteague will produce a foal at any given year. But in the Maryland portion of the island, where the mares continue to nurse their young, only 45% will foal at any given year.

The first year of life is the most dangerous for the colts. It has been estimated that 20% to 25% of the foals die within a year of birth.

When storms come, the horses move to the thickest part of the forest. When a hurricane gets at its worst, they lie down close to the ground.

During the summers of 1989 and 1990, approximately 40 Assateague wild horses died from Eastern Equine Encephalitis (EEE). This is a viral disease which attacks the nervous system of both horses and humans. It is usually deadly to both. The primary carrier of this disease to Assateague is believed to be the glossy ibis. Then it is transferred from the birds to the horses by mosquitoes. Apparently the disease is always present, but during those two years, the infestation of mosquitoes was even worse than usual. First the infected horses lost control of their muscles, then developed tremors, and finally died. Since the lactating mares and old harem stallions were the weakest, they died first.

In 1988 Dr. Jay Kirkpatrick and Dr. Alen Rutberg introduced a new approach to the fertility problem of the wild horses. A hormonal drug was administered to the mares which made them immune to their own eggs. The vaccine was given by small darts which meant they did not have to handle the horses. It was found to be better than 95% effective. And the vaccine's effect is believed to be reversible. If it is done correctly it should cause no permanent damage to the mare. The vaccine is not expensive and does not pass through the food chain, so if the animal dies and the dead body is consumed by another animal, it leaves no effect.

Studies are now being done to discover the long-term effects of the drug.

This has solved the population problem in the Maryland side of Assateague Island, keeping the size to the optimum 150 animals.

In Maryland, the ponies are free to roam and can be seen anywhere. It is suggested that you drive along roads and park in designated areas.

The parking lot at the Old Ferry landing and all along the beach are also good viewing areas.

In Virginia the horses can be seen in the fenced marshes south of the Beach Road and from the observation platform on the Woodland Trail.

The Chincoteague Fire Company, owners of the Virginia herd, are allowed grazing rights under a special permit issued by the Chincoteague National Wildlife Refuge. The Virginia herd is usually referred to as the Chincoteague ponies.

For years the Virginia herd population has been kept under strict control by yearly pennings and auctions. This herd is also limited to 150 animals. For years this was the only regular pony pennings held in North Carolina and Virginia for the sale of horses.

The mischievous ponies had no respect for the split log fences (sometimes called "worm fences")constructed by the early settlers.The ponies considered every vegetable garden and corn field on Chincoteague their own private dinner table. Because of this, about the beginning of the 18th century, the island men began an annual round-up and sale. At that time, it was generally believed that any ponies found on a man's land belonged to him.

These ponies were solid-colored bays, blacks, and sorrels with heavy curly manes and long silky tails. Their beauty was so well-known that when a pony penning was scheduled, people flocked to the island any way possible.

The first round-up and pony pennings were only attended by men; women were allowed to prepare the food, but take no part in the fun. Food and whiskey were plentiful and free. Ex-slaves did the roping and branding, riding the ponies bareback, using a wicket or rope for a bridle. The horses were rounded up, branded, then some were sold. It was a day of fellowship and fun.

In 1920 the town of Chincoteague suffered serious fires, one of which destroyed 2 homes and one in 1924 which destroyed most of the buildings on the west side of town. In May 1924, the Volunteer Fire Co. was organized with 14 members. They raised $4.16 by "pasing the hat." This was used to purchase stationary. In July a carnival was held, sposored by the Fire Company to raise money to buy equipment.

The Firemen puschased 80 ponies and established their own herd. The carnival has been held almost every year since its enception and has given the Fire Department financial stability. It is held on the last Wednesday and Thursday of July.

Chincoteague "cowboys" round up the Virginia herd for a spectacular swim across the channel to Chicoteague on Wednesday before thousands of cheering onlookers. On Thursday most of the foals and yearlings are auctioned off. The average bid for a pony is $225. The next day the remaining ponies cross back to Assateague
for another year.

Occasionally ponies may be seen begging or taking food from picnickers, but these ponies are wild and should be treated as such. While they may appear docile, sometimes even friendly, they are unpredictable and can inflict serious wounds by kicking and biting. Visitors are asked not to feed the ponies.

In the late 1970s, 40 California mustangs were brought to be introduced into the Virginia herd to improve breeding stock. Because they could not adjust to the hot, humid, insect-ridden summer and harsh, severe winter, most of them died during the first year.

Ponies that are sick or weak will not survive to produce healthy offspring and a strong, vital population. Sometimes action is taken to end the suffering of a seriously ill or dying pony, but no extraordinary measures are taken to prolong life.

Usually Assateague Island is able to withstand the force of the Atlantic storms. But sometimes when a hurricane comes barreling in, water is driven far inshore. The ponies and other wildlife must seek shelter on higher ground. The problem is that the high ground is only a few feet above sea level. Horses trying to reach the high sand dunes don't always make it. They have to swim for their lives. Some drown.

Plans are to continue careful management, to allow ponies to live wild and free on both ends of Assateague Island, a special treat for the pleasure of those who enjoy watching horses live untamed and untrained.

Ocracoke Ponies
Courtesy of © 1997 Ed Sanseverino
The Lighthouse Trading Post

CEDAR ISLAND

All of North Carolina's wild ponies did not live on government preserves. Several groups were privately owned and allowed to exist in a wild or semi-wild state. One such herd was on Cedar Island in Carteret County.

Cedar Island is a small fishing community of about 300 people, connected to the mainland by a high-rise modern bridge. The first record of settlement was in the early 1700s, but folks tell us that people lived there long before that.

The island has three churches, a community center, several stores, a post office, a motel-restaurant-gift shop, a campground and the state-owed ferry landing, connecting Cedar Island to Ocracoke.

Most of the island is not inhabited by man but is salt marsh, a part of the Cedar Island Wildlife Refuge.

There were horses on Cedar Island as far back as anyone can remember. When the first white folks came to live on the island they found small feral ponies, descended from Spanish horses who came ashore long ago from wrecked ships. Horses also lived on Hog Island, Harbor Island, and Chainshott Isles.

By 1800 all of the ponies were owned by the various families and carried their brand. Some were kept near the homes to be used to haul wood, to ride and to plow gardens. Others were put over on Core Banks where they ran wild. At the north end of Cedar Island, some were allowed to run with cattle.

When the law insisted that the horses be removed from Core Banks, some were sold while others joined the cattle on the north end of the island.

The first round-ups or pony pennings were held to brand the colts and perhaps to sell one or two. Since that time a few larger domesticated horses were added to the herd. Some died, but others survived. Because of this the ponies became somewhat larger than those in the herds located at some other places along the Carolina Banks. In the spring and summer of 1949 (before television came to the island), men from both Roe and Lola gathered at the north end of the island almost every week to round-up the horses that had run wild in the woods all winter. This strenuous activity took place every sunny Sunday just for the sport of it.

The beaters usually started out after the horses early in the morning. Some beaters rode their own horses in the round-up. No fancy leather saddles for these cowboys; they tossed burlap bags across the backs of their mounts, grabbed rope or leather bridles, mounted up and galloped away southward to begin the round-up.

The horses were driven to the north end of the island into a barbed wire fence enclosure which stretched west from the pen straight east and out into Pamlico Sound. It was necessary for the fence to reach out into the Sound to prevent the animals from dashing out into the water and around the end, thus escaping the penning grounds.

By noon a crowd had gathered in the vicinity of the pen. Each spectator present hoped to be the first one to catch sight of the flowing manes above the high marsh grasses, a sign that the horses were coming.

At the end of the drive, the drivers on horseback were joined by men and boys standing outside the fence, screaming loud Indian-like yells at the ponies as they thundered by and were maneuvered into the enclosure.

Once inside the pen, the horses milled around, docile for the most part. After the ponies were penned, the beaters brought in the second group which had escaped during the first drive.

On one Sunday, the spectators were treated to

a stallion fight which held them spellbound. And nervous.

Spring is the time of the mating season. Being closely confined in the pen brings out the winter-dormant instincts. Each gang of eight to 12 mares was led by one dominant stallion. On this particular Sunday, a younger, smaller, dun-colored stallion challenged the older leader.

It began by stooping and sniffing, then proceeded to head-touching, head shaking and loud neighing. Then the younger stallion kicked the larger one in the chest. At last their heads locked in a neck-biting frenzy, rolling and kicking with all eight hooves. The larger, older stallion was the winner; the challenger retreated, perhaps to fight again the next mating season.

Neither stallion was seriously injured.

At these horse pennings, the average number of horses taken each Sunday was about 12, but the men claimed that there were between 15 and 20 others so wild and cunning they were never caught.

By the time six or eight Sundays had passed, the horses which had been turned loose each Sunday evening, came to know what day of the week it was, so when they saw the men coming, they obediently began the trek towards the pen.

There was one wild stallion that the penners were trying to get hold of, but hadn't managed to catch. The men used this stallion as their excuse to continue the weekly round-ups.

The area where these horses ran was made up of sand dunes, marshes, small inlets and woods, extending from Hog Island to Whaler's Camp, a channel between Harbor Island and Chainshott Isles. There were pot holes which contained fresh water.

Many of the horses belonged to Eugene Styron.

According to Mr. Styron the horses were similar to those on Carrot Island. Mr. Styron sold horses to individuals and to groups who wanted to add to their herds.

He said that his grandfather Daniel Eugene Styron told him that at one time there were between 600 to 700 horses roaming on that end of the island. At pony pennings some of the horses were picked out to be gentled, tamed, and used to plow gardens, pull carts, or to haul wood. Stallions not wanted for breeding purposes were sometimes gelded.

Mr. Styron told about the time Mr. Winfield Daniels, a Cedar Island businessman, decided to go into the horse business. "Mr. Daniels had some really nice wooden water boxes built. Then he drove a well down and hooked up a gas motor to furnish water for his horses. But the horses refused to drink water from his fine wooden boxes. They didn't know how. The only water they knew came from the ground."

Mr. Styron chuckled. "Mr. Daniels should of saved his money, bought 'em a shovel and dug a hole."

"Guess he discovered the old saying 'You can take a horse to water, but you can't make him drink,'came from someone dealing with marsh ponies."

When the motel next to the ferry terminal was first opened, employees complained about the wild horses which roamed freely, messing up the place. Guests objected to being awakened by wild horses galloping by. In order to avoid problems, many of the islanders sold their horses. Then the management of the motel had a tall fence built at the edge of the campground to keep the horses away.

Near the ferry landing, Mr. Cato, an "outsider," came down and opened a riding stable. He kept domesticated horses to rent out and stabled horses for others who wanted to ride along the beach.

In the fall of 1996, trouble came. It was discovered that horses belonging to the stable tested positive to EIA. After some discussion about having the infected horses isolated some place else, they were destroyed.

The stable was closed until further notice.

The question as to how the horses were exposed to the disease was a puzzler.

Even the state authorities had to admit that the horses at Shackleford were too far away to be involved. It was possible that a domestic horse brought to ride along the sandy, uncluttered beach had brought the disease.

Efforts were made to contact the owners whose horses had been brought to Cedar Island during that period.

"We tested all the horses we could find and did not find any positive (for the disease)," Mr. Cato said. Apparently he did not locate them all.

Other domesticated horses on the island were also tested. They proved to be healthy and free of the disease.

Testing of all these horses accomplished two

things—it eliminated them as the carriers of the disease and meant they had not been infected from the stable horses.

The stable was a considerable distance from where the wild horses roamed, but people sometimes rode their domesticated horses on the beach near there.

The wild horses lived on the 18 mile-long Cedar Island Beach and its 2,000 surrounding acres of marsh, woods, and islets.

In February of 1997 state vet Dr. Andy Mixson directed the round up the herd of wild horses. But they only caught five. According to Mixson, they tested positive and were killed and buried at the site.

This left seven horses they were unable to catch. Since they could also test positive, infecting other horses, they too had to be tested. One mare had delivered a foal, so now there were believed to be eight horses to consider. Spring brought on another mosquito season and increased the danger of the EIA disease being spread.

The people on Cedar Island objected to having an outsider come in and tell them what to do. The state did not own the horses. Nor the land they lived on. And horses had been there many generations before the riding stable was even thought of.

At first the Cedar Islanders refused to cooperate with the state. Years ago, all wild or semi-wild horses were branded, but these weren't. No one claimed ownership. The original owners and horses had died. The state authorities said whoever owned the ponies would be responsible for the cost of the round up.

The State quarantined that end of Cedar Island and threatened to quarantine the entire island if the wild horses were not caught and tested. This would have meant that any horses brought on the island would have to remain quarantined for 60 days, and no horses could be taken off the island even to go to horse shows or the vet.

Some of the Cedar Islanders capitulated. They went out by foot and in four-wheel vehicles and rounded up the remaining horses, knowing full well that the horses would probably be killed. They found nine.

Dr. Mixson announced that seven of them tested positive. Without consulting Cedar Islanders, the horses were "euthanized."

Keelie Gaskill, one of the Cedar Islanders who fought for the ponies, said, "After they were all rounded up, I went down the beach to where they were penned and took videos of two beautiful dun colored stallions, a two-month old sorrel filly and five other healthy horses on the beach. They watched us nervously and crowded round the filly trying to protect her while she peeked around their legs, curiously."

When Keelie returned the following evening, she was locked out but she could see men dragging the dead bodies to an 18-wheeler and dumping them in the back of it.

Mixon stated, "The horses euthanized Thursday were taken to a rendering facility, where they were to be disposed of in a manner much like cremation. Bone meal and other remains from animals disposed of at such facilities is sometimes used for animal feed or fertilizer."

They call it "euthanized," a euphemism for murder.

A soft word does not change a fact. Horses have feelings. They know each other and care for each other. When one is stuck in the mud, others close in to try to help. When one dies, the loss is felt by all. The grief of the survivors is very real. The authorities allowed two mares to survive, at least for now. One is a yearling and the other a two or three year old. Two young mares does not a herd make.

Keelie felt that the two month-old filly should have been taken care of until her mother's antibodies had washed through her system and would have tested negative. It is difficult to understand how any human being could kill a baby if there was any way it could have been saved.

So the government accomplished in less than six months what 450 years of fighting wolves and disease and hurricanes and drought and insects could not.

The wild horses on Cedar Island are no more. All that remains are the memories.

Cedar Island Ponies June 12, 1997
The day before their execution.
Keelie Gaskill

Cedar Island Ponies June 12, 1997
The day before their execution.
Keelie Gaskill

Shackleford Ponies
Robert Day

Cedar Island Ponies
Courtesy of Eugene Styron

WESTERN WILD HORSES

In times past, thousands of mustangs could be heard thundering across the Western plains. They still remain but in much smaller numbers.

They, like those found on the Outer Banks, are descended from horses brought to the New World by Spanish explorers hundreds of years ago. But these came primarily from explorers and into Mexico. When ranchers and farmers moved in, they brought their own domesticated horses.

Some of these joined the wild herds.

When speaking of the western wild horses, the term mustang is used generically. The word "mustang" is the English pronunciation of the Spanish word "mesteno" meaning stray or wild. These horses are generally smaller than the usual domestic horse because of their Spanish heritage and the lack of proper food.

While in the east, the Indians seldom rode horses, in the west, they adopted the horse, which was there for the catching. Much has been said about the Indians stealing the ranchers' horses, but the truth is the white men stole more of the Indians' steeds than the Indian the whites'. These horses were an important part of the Old West; the cavalry battles of the Civil War, Pony Express and stage coaches. And of course the cowboy. Riding one of these fast, intelligent horses was the best means to handle the cattle from the 1860s on.

Then came modernization. The horses became less necessary. Gasoline-powered automobiles and buses and farm equipment made the horse obsolete.

This meant the horses were either pets or pests, depending on one's point of view.

Mustangs live in ten western states, but mostly in Nevada. Herds of from 1,500 to 4,000 live in Idaho, Oregon, Wyoming, Colorado, New Mexico, and California. Smaller numbers live in Montana, Utah, and Arizona. By 1860, the mustang population had reached an estimated two million.

Farmers and ranchers were angry because they claimed that the hordes of horses were eating the grass and drinking the water that belonged to THEIR cattle and destroying the land. They claimed that mustang stallions were breaking down fences and stealing their mares.

The BLM (Bureau of Land Management) is in charge of government lands, where farmers pay a nominal fee for their livestock to graze.

The wild horses must share this area with the ranchers' cattle and sheep, mining, logging, and recreation activities.

When the ranchers complained about the horses, the BLM told them if they didn't like it, to get rid of them. And they did. Many hired wild-horse hunters (mustangers) to solve their problem. Thousands of mustangs were killed. Others were rounded up and sold to slaughter-houses, hide buyers, chicken-feed factories, and pet-food canneries. County governments, run by ranchers, supported the slaughter. In fact, ranchers and mustangers were paid two dollars for each pair of horses' ears they turned in.

Americans have always refused to eat horse meat, but Europeans were never that particular. Millions of pounds of horse meat went to Europe.

A favorite way to corral the horses was to chase them into a dead-end canyon or hidden corral and roped one at a time. Another way was with a box trap on a trail used by horse bands. The box was buried and covered by leaves and tied to a stone or log. When the horse stepped into the trap, it was caught by the foot. Sometimes traps were built around waterholes or springs. A gate fell into place when the horses went in for water.

But then the mustangers discovered the airplane. From the air it was easier to spot the roaming herds. They flew in low and fired gunshots at the horses, who would leave their hiding places and run into the open where trucks waited for them. Some were shot, others died from exhaustion.

Once corralled, the horses piled up and sometimes trampled each other to death. In the truck they were taken for long trips, packed tightly together, and given no food or water, causing injuries and deaths.

In 1950 Velma Johnson was driving toward Reno, Nevada, when she saw a truckload of wild horses ahead of her. The truck dribbled a streak of a guey substance on the road. She stopped the truck, thinking it could have a serious problem.

Mrs. Johnson couldn't believe what she saw. Blood was everywhere. The horses were packed in tight as sardines. A colt lay dead on the floor where it had been trampled. Others suffered from gunshot wounds. A stallion's eyes had been shot out. She was appalled, "How did these horses get in such horrible condition?"

"They were shot from an airplane," the driver answered.

Mrs. Johnson decided that she had to do something to halt this atrocious practice. When she complained to the BLM, she was ignored. When she figured they were in cahoots with the mustangers. So she started a crusade to protect the wild horses.

She was soon nicknamed "Wild Horse Annie."

She was proud of the name and from then on, adopted it as her own. In 1952, because of her politicking, Story County, Nevada made it illegal to chase wild horses by plane.

She continued writing magazine articles, circulating petitions, and writing letters to newspapers, humane organizations, and to prominent citizens. In 1955 a bill similar to the one passed in Story County was passed by the state of Nevada.

Annie reaized that Nevada was not the only place this murderous act was sanctioned.

She sent photographs and detailed descriptions of horse hunting to Congressmen and Senators. In 1959 Congress passed a law making it a felony to use airplanes and motorized vehicles to round up unbranded wild horses on public lands. This was the first federal law to protect wild horses.

Their number dwindled from an estimated two million in 1860 to 17,000 mustangs in 1970.

It was in the early 1970s that the American people, especially the school children became concerned about the plight of the mustangs.

Animal groups were certain that within a decade the wild horse, a symbol of American history, would be extinct. The Federal program was discussed on radio and TV and in schools throughout the nation. Congress received thousands of letters concerning the problem.

In 1971 Congress passed the Wild Free-Roaming Horse and Burro Act, making it illegal to harass or kill wild horses or burros on public lands.

Then in a few years, the ranchers were again complaining to the BLM about the rapidly increasing herds of wild horses. They claimed the population rose as much as 20 per cent a year. Pressure was applied to the BLM.

For the horses' protection, new legislation set up an Adopt-A-Horse program, a good idea but with its own problems. The BLM rounded up thousands of horses to be adopted. In the beginning many were injured or killed during the round-up.

As time passed, they became more efficient with fewer casualties. Homes were found for many wild horses. Others were placed in private sanctuaries to be used in experimental fertility programs.

Since those wanted for adoption were young, removing them meant the mares were free to become pregnant again. The problem of the mustangs was a never ending one.

The Adopt-a-Horse program came under fire because of possible violations of its intent.

Under the program's rules, anyone who was eligible could adopt up to four horses a year if they could prove they could adequately provide acreage, food and care for them. They paid $125 for each horse. At the end of a year, if a veterinarian certified that the horse was well taken care of, the new owner got legal title, a handsome certificate containing the identification number freeze-branded on the horse's hide.

Europeans paid a high price for horse meat. At the end of the first year, the owner is free to sell the animal. Many did. Allegations were also made that members of families connected

with the program bought horses, intending to
sell them later for horse meat.

The multi-million dollar government adoption
program, intended to save the lives of wild
horses was instead sending many of them into
slaughter houses.

The Bureau of Land Management plans to round
up as many as 10,000 wild horses this year.
The National Park Service shot and killed over
400 burros between 1987 and 1995 in Death Valley
National Park. They now plan to round up over
1,000 more in the Mojave National Preserve.

Using whatever pretense they can dream up,
the government programs which oversee government
lands--the National Park Service, the US Forest
Service, and the military are destroying the
wild horses and burros.

According to Susan Wagner, president of the
"Equine Advocates, Inc.," the various government
agencies are consistently favoring big business
interests to the detriment of our wild horses.
This is true in the West as well as in the East.

What is the solution to the problem out West?
Everyone has different ideas, depending upon
their agendas. Since the horses belong to the
government--the people--if there is not enough
forage for both cattle and horses, denying the
almost free land to the ranchers is one solution.
This is highly unlikely.

Animal protection groups argue that livestock
outnumbers mustangs by more than 100 to one,
and livestock are more likely to cause damage
to the land than horses. Some ecologists say
the money spent to manage mustangs should be

spent protecting endangered species.

The wild horse is already an endangered species in the East and if the ranchers have their way, is in danger of becoming one in the West.

Ocracoke Ponies
Courtesy of © 1997 Ed Sanseverino
The Lighthouse Trading Post

THE FUTURE OF THE BANKER PONIES

The Banker ponies are an endangered species. And the land upon which they dwell is an endangered land.

At one time, thousands of these small tough ponies roamed over the barrier islands nourished by and nourishing the land.

Because of man's encroachment upon their territory, they are now penned in with no place for their normal increase. We would like to think of them wild and free, running with the wind, splashing in the sound, untamed and unfenced.

But times have changed. The land has changed until now we must accept with grace what has gone before and do the best we can for both the ponies and the land which remains.

As cities and towns and communities grew, there is little of nature left to be seen. Children grow up and die, never having seen animals in the wild. Being allowed to observe these magnificent stallions with their families munching on marsh grass or galloping along the shore fulfills a need in us all.

Because there are—or were—seven different herds with seven different caretakers, it is important to consider each herd separately.

The horses at Assateague are under the management of the Assateague Island Seashore. The herd is stabilized at 150 horses, the number the land can safely support. By utilizing a proven birth control method, the herd remains within that number. The Assateague Seashore is dedicated to caring for both the land and the horses.

At Chincoteague, the Chincoteague Fire Department, who owns the horses, also keeps their herd at approximately 150 animals. By the judicious use of yearly auctions, their herd has remained both healthy and profitable.

From the 5,000 to 6,000 ponies found on the Sand Banks of North Carolina in 1926, the number has now dwindled to less than 300. This is a gigantic tragedy.

Although the ponies are no longer necessary for heavy work, they are still an important part of our heritage.

At Corolla, two large healthy herds have been reduced to approximately 42 animals running on a huge expanse of government and privately owned land. The horses are under the management of the Corolla Wild Horse Fund, an active, dedicated group interested in caring for the ponies. By diligent politicking and hours of personal work, they have prevented the deaths of innumerable animals. At the present time, the herd is stable. The problem is that the government objects to having the horses on their land, and the private land is in danger of being developed.

The ponies on Carrot Island, across from Beaufort have undergone traumatic changes, many deaths from starvation and parasites, then by the state, who manages the herd. Because of the small number of horses remaining and the use of birth control, this herd will take close monitoring by the people of Beaufort to insure that the indiscriminate use of birth control does not destroy the herd.

The horses at Ocracoke is a fine example of a managed herd. It is semi-wild under the auspices of the National Park Service. The park rangers care for the herd much like domesticated horses. The result is a small herd closely resembling the ones Barlowe and Amandas found when they came ashore in 1584.

The latest tragedy is what happened on Cedar Island. This was a private herd on private land. Because the EIA disease was found in horses at a riding stable on that end of the island, the state insisted the wild herd be tested. They found 12 horses testing positive and had them killed. This left two young mares. So the wild horse herd on Cedar Island is completely decimated.

When the people of North Carolina think of the wild ponies they think of the Shackleford ponies. It was a large herd. In spite of the loud objections of the local people, the Cape Lookout National Seashore removed and killed 76 horses because of the EIA disease. Since Shackleford Banks is well beyond the distance required by law for isolation of this disease, this was seen as both unnecessary and vengeful. Experts say that horses on islands such as Shackleford have had this disease for many generations and have become almost immune to its consequences. Because of the diligent activism of the Foundation for Shackleford Horses, the number saved is reasonable for the land space. If the care is turned over to the Foundation, in spite of opposition by the Cape Lookout National Seashore, there is every reason to believe that ponies on Shackleford can remain one of Carteret County's major tourist attractions.

Although for many years, scientists claimed the Banker ponies were exotic, they are not. They are feral, descended from horses brought to the New World by the Spanish over 400 years ago. Surely that is sufficient time to establish them the right to exist in small numbers, unshackled by civilization.

Ocracoke Ponies
Courtesy of © 1997 Ed Sanseverino
The Lighthouse Trading Post

ORGANIZATIONS:

Corolla Wild Horse Fund of
    Outer Banks Conservtionists
    PO Box 361
    Corolla NC 27927
Equine Advocates
    Susan Wagner
    Suite 185
    76-04 Main St
    Flushing NY 11367 (718) 897-9422
Foundation for Shackleford Horses
    PO Box 841
    Beaufort NC 28512
Hooved Animal Protection Society
    Dept HI
    10804 McConnel Rd
    Woodstock IL 60098-0400
The Large Animal Protection Society
    Dept HI
    PO Box 223
    Parkesburg PA 19365
    ****
American Feral Horse Association
    4820 Allamar
    Boise ID 83704 (208) 375-1384
American Mustang Association
    PO Box 338
    Yucaipa CA 92399
American Mustang & Burro Association Inc
    PO Box 788
    Lincoln CA 95648 (916) 633-9271

American Mustang & Burro Association Inc
      PO Box 216
      Liberty Hill TX 78642 (800) US-4-WILD
Bureau of Land Management
National Wild Horse and Burro Program Office
      850 Harvard Way
      PO Box 12000
      Reno NV 89520-0006 (702) 785-6583
Friends of the Mustangs
      c/o Judy Cady
      2131 L-1/2 Road
      Grand Junction CO 81505
International Society for the Protection
      of Mustangs & Burros (ISPMB)
      6212 East Sweetwater Ave
      Scottsdale AZ 85254 (602)991-0273
Middle Tennessee Mustang Association
      PO Box 1671
      Lavergne TN 37086 (615) 793-3776
National Mustang Orgnization Inc
      1st and Main Streets
      Newcastle UT 84756 (801) 439-5440
National Organization for Wild Horses Inc
      1330 South 9th St
      Canon City CO 81212 (719)275-1142
North American Mustang Association & Registry
      PO Box 850906
      Mesquite TX 75185-0906 (214) 289-9344
Steens Mountain Kiger Registry
      26450 Horsell
      Bend OR 97701 (541) 389-3895
Tri-State Mustang Club
      RR1 Box 180
      Hayfield MN 55940 (507) 477-2676

BIBLIOGRAPHY   141

A Survey History of Cape Lookout National
Seashore.

Assateague Island, "The Wild Ponies," National
Park Services, US Dept of the Interior.

Assateague Island, Assateague Island National
Seashore, Maryland and Virginia. National Park
Service, US Dept of Interior.

Balance Alton, Ocracokers, U of NC Press, Chapel
Hill NC, 1989.

Brown Cindy Kilgore, "Wild Horses of the Outer
Banks," Triology, Sept, Oct 1992.

Carteret County, a Compiled History, East
Carteret High School, Beaufort NC 1982.

Exploration, Descriptions and Attempted
Settlement of Carolina, NC State Archives and
History, 1953.

Hyde County North Carolina, Genealogy, Hyde
County History; A Hyde County Bicentennial
project, Hyde County Historical Society, 1976.

Hyde County, A New Geography.

Kirkpatrick Jay F, Into the Wind, Wild Horses
of North America, NorthWord Press Inc, Minocqua
WI, 1994.

National Geographic Magazine, May, 1926.

Outer Banks Magazine 1995-96.

"Journal of the Corolla," edited by Angel Ellis Khoury.

Rood, Ronald, Hundred Acre Welcome, 1967, Stephen Green Press, Vermont.

Stick David, North Carolina Lighthouse, NC Dept of Culural Resourse, Div of Archives and History, Raleigh NC 1981.

Stick David, The Outer Banks of North Carolina, University of North Carolina, 1958.

Numerous articles from the following newspapers 1959-1997.

Carteret County News Times, Morehead City NC.
Daily News, Jacksonville, NC.
Eastern Weekly, Beaufort NC.
News and Observer, Raleigh NC.
Sun Journal, New Bern, NC.
Washington Post, Wash DC.

Information from:
Assateague Island, National Seashore, MD.
Cape Hatteras National Seashore, NC.
Cedar Island Wildlife Refuge, NC.
Chincoteague Fire Department, VA.
Cumberland Island National Seashore, GA.
Currituck Co Wildlife Horse Sanctuary, NC. 1997.
U of Kentucky, College of Ag, Vet Service, 1993.
TV News at WCTI, New Bern NC.